Endeavours to Mend

Perspectives on British Quaker work in the world today

True godliness don't turn men out of the world but enables them to live better in it and excites their endeavours to mend it.

William Penn, 1682

Endeavours to Mend

Perspectives on British Quaker work
in the world today

Edited by Brian Phillips with John Lampen

QUAKERbooks

First published 2006 by Quaker Books

Friends House, 173 Euston Road, London NW1 2BJ

www.quaker.org.uk

ISBN 0 85245 388 4

PHOTO CREDITS:

Cover: Photo © John Crawford
Page 12: Photo © John Crawford
Page 20: Photo © John Lampen
Page 29: Photos (top) © John Lampen
   (bottom) © Peter Daniels
Page 39: Photo © Library of the Religious Society
   of Friends, London
Page 44: Photo © Bahati Muhesi
Page 54: Photo © Graham Nunn
Page 60: Photo © Kwaku Amponah
Page 65: Photo © Chris Hunter
Page 73: Photo © Daimokh
Page 83: Photo © International Labour Organization
Page 101: Photo © Paul Dix/QPSW
Page 106: Photo © Matt Robson
Page 111: Photo © Ida Suhrke
Page 116: Photo © Jeanne Coker

Printed and bound in Great Britain by Biddles Ltd, King's Lynn, Norfolk

Contents

Acknowledgements

I am deeply grateful to the many individuals who have made contributions to this book. Rachel Brett, Rachel Carmichael, Diana Francis, Chris Hunter, Diana and John Lampen, Grigor McClelland, and Robin Robison have generously shared their thinking in a series of stimulating chapters. Additional thanks to John Lampen for his unfailing support for the idea of this collection and for his steadfast editorial and logistical assistance. Peter Daniels of Quaker Books has helpfully guided the book to publication.

The catalyst for this book was my experience as a Joseph Rowntree Quaker Fellow during 2001 02, when I had an extraordinary opportunity to reflect on the subject of Quaker global witness with Friends throughout the country in a series of presentations and workshops. I am grateful to the Joseph Rowntree Charitable Trust for making this possible, and for the Trust's enthusiastic embrace of my Fellowship programme. My Fellowship year and my continuing work in this area have also been wonderfully supported by Oxford Meeting throughout the past four years.

I also wish to thank numerous staff of Quaker Peace & Social Witness (and its predecessor Quaker Peace & Service) as well as the membership of a variety of oversight committees serving these bodies. Their friendship, teaching and inspiration over the past decade have certainly informed this project on many levels.

While the scope of the book is limited to recent examples of Quaker global witness arising within Britain Yearly Meeting (apart from the chapter on the Quaker United Nations Office, Geneva) I also wish to recognise here the vital contributions to the contemporary renewal of that tradition by other yearly meetings of the Religious Society of Friends worldwide. I hope that this volume may encourage at least some of them to produce similar publications exploring their own current work in this area.

Finally, although the focus of this book is Quaker witness on the world stage, the principles and insights discussed here will of course have great resonance for work being undertaken by Friends at the national and local level as well. I trust that this book will help us to better appreciate the continuum of Quaker service wherever it is carried out – both corporately and individually – by faithful Friends committed to the mending of Creation.

Brian Phillips
Oxford, August 2005

Chapter 1

Quaker Global Witness
in the Twenty-first Century

by Brian Phillips

I want to begin this chapter with a tale of two incidents from a single city in the Balkans. On Monday 7 May 2001 a group of Bosnian Muslims and various representatives of both the international community and the Bosnian Serb government gathered in the city of Banja Luka (capital of Republika Srpska, the Serbian entity of Bosnia-Herzegovina) to begin the long awaited reconstruction of the city's most historic mosque. It was exactly eight years to the day that the sixteenth-century Ferhadija Mosque had been blown up by Bosnian Serb extremists in 1993 – one of sixteen mosques in Banja Luka destroyed in an effort to erase these symbols of the city's centuries-old Islamic culture.

As local police stood by, around 2000 people sought to disrupt the ceremony with anti-Islamic slogans and songs. And then the crowd turned violent. Stones were thrown at Muslim participants arriving for the ceremony. Seven buses that had brought these visitors to the city were duly set on fire. A number of elderly men were attacked as the demonstrators broke through the police cordon. Thirty people were injured in the assault – and one man subsequently died as a result of his injuries.

The Muslim flag on the Islamic community centre was pulled down and burned and a Bosnian Serb flag defiantly hung in its place. The crowd also herded a pig to the site of the old mosque, where they proceeded to butcher the animal and hang its head up for public display. Even more disturbing than the presence of Bosnian Serb nationalist politicians and army veterans among the crowd was the fact that schoolchildren were reported to have been at the forefront of this appalling scene (Gordana Katana 2001).

For anyone who has sought to help build a culture of peace, justice and human rights in Bosnia in recent years, this incident could easily be seen as a mark of our collective failure to stem the tide of hatred and violence in the region. And yet I found strength enough to resist that temptation to despair by recalling another story from Banja Luka. It is a story that quite literally happened just down the road from the terrible scene I have described, exactly one month earlier on 6 April 2001. On that date Quaker Peace & Social Witness (QPSW) held the first ever "Quaker Roundtable" in the Balkans in the very same city.

In a modest way, it felt as if we were making Quaker history. This was a unique opportunity for deepening the spiritual relationship of Britain Yearly Meeting (BYM) with the Bosnian partner organisations of our QPSW Sarajevo Programme. We had been careful to emphasise that our aim in convening the roundtable was not to proselytise but to inform. We began by asking each of the participants to tell us something of their experience with Quakers in Bosnia thus far and their understanding of the Quaker faith. We also asked them to spell out what it was that they most wanted to learn from the day.

Some said they were eager to hear more about Quaker history, expressing curiosity about the Society's origins and its evolution over the centuries. Others wanted to know more about the roots of our commitment to nonviolence or about our relationship to other branches of the Christian church and to other religious traditions. One participant talked of how his passion for American films as a child had brought about his first contact with Friends. He recalled that the character played by Grace Kelly in the famous Gary Cooper film *High Noon* had been a Quaker. Another confessed to his persistent confusion between the words "Quaker" and "cracker" when grappling with the English language.

Nothing testifies more vividly to the genuine spiritual power of the gathering than some of the comments made at the close of the day. In the light of what they had learned about Quaker history and the testimonies, we asked these young people to tell us what it was they would be taking away from the roundtable.

One activist from a nongovernmental organisation (NGO) in Tuzla – from a background of mixed nationality – said that learning about our silent meeting for worship had taken her back to a time during the war when she had been very much alone. It was a time when she had had to reach deep inside herself to find the strength that enabled her to go on living. She told us she'd been struck by the similarity of her own experience to the Quaker understanding of the Inner Light. An activist from a Sarajevo nongovernmental organisation engaged in training for nonviolence said that at least two or three times during the day he had thought to himself: "I am a Quaker."

Among participants from Republika Srpska, a youth activist from Srpsko Sarajevo said that the day had brought her an awareness of things she had never faced before. Hearing about the Inner Light had helped her to recognise that this is the source from which she operates in her own life. Another young man from Banja Luka – courageously working to promote the right to conscientious objection to military service there – expressed regret that there had not been any Quaker presence in Bosnia earlier. He speculated about the impact Quakers might have made in the country had they been present at the start of the 1990s. And he wondered aloud what Bosnia might be like if it were to become a "Quaker state" where everyone lived in accordance with the testimonies.

A youth activist from a small town in Eastern Bosnia said that she'd recently seen the film *Gladiator* and that this violent film's popularity had upset her greatly. She had begun to conclude that human beings love violence and that this attraction is something deep within them. The Banja Luka Quaker roundtable had been like a "sign" to her – a realisation that there is an opposing force in the world that is against violence.

For me personally the roundtable was one of the most profound experiences of my life as a Quaker. Rarely have I felt what Isaac Penington described as the "quickenings and pressings" of the Spirit so intensely as I did in this remarkable gathering. Any apprehension we had felt about appearing to evangelise was quickly dispelled by the evident relish with which participants engaged with what we had to offer them. We left with a sense that a vital, viable model for international outreach had emerged from this event – one that might soon be extended to other partners working for peace, human rights and social justice elsewhere in the region.

I begin with these twin tales from Banja Luka because I believe they testify to the enduring power and contemporary relevance of our Quaker global witness. I believe that the work we as Quakers are carrying out in places like Bosnia today – chiefly through the support of local actors whom we believe to be a leaven for the transformation of their conflict-ridden societies – is nothing less than proof positive that there is indeed, as George Fox wrote in the seventeenth century, "an infinite ocean of light and love" flowing over "the ocean of darkness and death" (*QFP* 19.03).

Every day we all struggle under the weight of the torrent of tragic news that so often seems to define our world. Yet I would argue that the authentic communion we experienced with these young Bosnians in April 2001 is as much the reality of our present global condition as the grim events that followed there a few weeks later. And I am quite convinced that without the catalyst of BYM's commitment to these young activists there might never have been a space in which those "quickenings and pressings" of the Spirit – those unmistakable intimations of the Kingdom of God – could have broken through into this violent world. To say this is not to make some un-Quakerly boast about our unique gifts as agents for social and political change, but

Burial of victims of 1995 Srebrenica massacres, Bosnia-Herzegovina, July 2005

rather to grasp what I believe to be nothing less than our spiritual responsibility.

I have little doubt then that at the start of the twenty-first century, Quaker global witness is alive and well and urgently needed in the world. But the continuing validity of that statement depends very much on our ability to recognise the distinctive qualities and the particular value of our contemporary witness. During the course of my Rowntree Quaker Fellowship in 2001–02, I sought to provide Friends in Britain Yearly Meeting with some fresh tools to discover for themselves how Quakerism and global work and witness can be seen as inseparable components of our faith. I wanted Friends to delight in the recognition that we have no choice but to be witnesses in the world to God's loving power – because we are Quakers. To paraphrase American theologian Stanley Hauerwas, the Society of Friends does not *have* an internationalist tradition, the Society of Friends *is* an internationalist tradition.

As that claim suggests, this understanding lies at the very heart of our Quaker identity, rooted deep in our seventeenth-century origins. It is a truth consistent with what Quaker historian Doug Gwyn has described as the way in which "Early Friends experienced the light not as a warm, cuddly inner teddy bear but as the risen Christ, the ultimate future, the destiny of the universe, breaking into the present" (Ben Pink Dandelion, Doug Gwyn & Timothy Peat 1998, p140). Theirs was a faith understood to be nothing less than "Christ speaking and acting through the lives of transformed men and women, Christ challenging the violent and unjust norms of an alienated society" (ibid).

Gwyn reminds us that this "return of Christ through the light or seed within was not a private, inward experience. It moved outward into society, into history, as men and women followed Christ in a new way of life" (ibid). Not a bad description, I think, of a truly dynamic Quaker global witness. But living as we do in a world and indeed in a Society of Friends that seems at times light years away from our seventeenth-century forebears, how can we generate a similar dynamism about a Quaker global witness for our own time?

During the course of my Fellowship, one of the ways in which I sought to re-engage local Friends with our tradition of global witness was to suggest to them a series of five qualities that might be said to characterise much of the international work that Quakers do today. This includes both corporate work (in places like the Balkans, Uganda, South Asia, Northern Ireland and Israel/Palestine) and the witness of individual Friends working under concern or as employees of any number of agencies for good. In discussing our tradition in relation to these five qualities, I did not wish to suggest that these characteristics or qualities are somehow uniquely Quaker – that is to say, that we are the only witnesses to justice and peace working in this way today. Many other international humanitarian, human rights and development agencies integrate these same insights and approaches into various aspects of their work. But as Quakers we are sometimes in a unique position to make such approaches a priority in our work in ways that larger, better-resourced actors frequently are not.

In arriving at these five particular defining qualities, I was effectively answering for myself a question I had often been asked by colleagues at Amnesty International during more than a decade of service with that organisation. They knew that I was a Friend and deeply involved in Quaker work in the Balkans (simultaneous with my Amnesty work in the region). I was often asked: "What is it that you Quakers are actually doing in Bosnia today? You're a small community with a glorious, pioneering tradition of international work behind you. You have been in the vanguard of so many of the movements that gave birth to the NGO giants of the second half of the twentieth century. But you haven't got much money now and you haven't got large numbers of staff to deploy in the field. Perhaps it's time to wrap it up – to leave this kind of work to the major players like Oxfam and Amnesty and Christian Aid?"

I must stress that my answer to these questions – in the form of what I have called the five distinctive qualities of contemporary Quaker global witness – reflects our aspirations as much as our actual accomplishments. Quakers can be as fallible as any human community intent upon doing good in the world, and we, too, sometimes fall short of the mark. But at the same time this list of five qualities is not just a catalogue of well meaning if vague wishes largely produced for our own consumption, as are the insubstantial "mission statements" of so many organisations today. My list is based upon specific responses articulated by some of the organisations and initiatives with whom we have been working in recent years. It reflects what our partners are telling us that they most value about their continuing association with the Religious Society of Friends and with individual Quakers. Naturally, my illustrations of these five points are drawn from my direct personal experience of the Balkans. But readers who have worked elsewhere as Friends will hopefully be able to draw immediate parallels with those places where they have sought to live their Quaker faith.

Identifying those who can make a change

The first of these five qualities which merits discussion is our sometimes uncanny ability as Friends, both corporately and individually, to identify those activists or initiatives best placed to help create a culture of peace, justice and human rights in a society marked by conflict or oppression. These are often individuals or groups who live and work on the margins of their society – people whose values and views may be in stark contrast with those of the majority. Because of their principles or convictions, these are people who may at best be regarded with suspicion by their own communities – and, at worst, as dangerous subversives whose opinions must be refuted or actively suppressed.

As individuals or small groups of like-minded people – sometimes little more than the embryo of what might with time become an initiative or organisation – these potential activists may be largely neglected or passed over by major funders and other international organisations who want first to see clear evidence of sound organisational structures or an identifiable local constituency. Discovering such people is often a matter of seeking out isolated or relatively inaccessible communities, far from the conveniences of a capital city. It requires an ability to work close to the ground in such places – to be alert to those developing alternative visions of a society and to those speaking a new and different language that may be regarded as alien by the surrounding culture.

Paradoxically, this is an area where the relatively small scale of much Quaker work may be a distinct advantage. In many ways, our size enables us to work more effectively in these settings – to do the kind of deep listening essential to the identification process discussed above. When QPSW was considering how best to contribute to post-conflict social reconstruction efforts in Bosnia in the second half of the 1990s, we spent the better part of a year doing nothing more than travelling around the country and listening to those voices (frequently in off-the-beaten-path places) who were speaking about the need for a transformation of their society. Before embarking on any kind of formal Quaker programme in the region, we felt it was of great importance to allow those pioneering voices to be heard and then to create our programme on the basis of the riches uncovered in local communities rather than adhering to any externally imposed framework.

A ministry of presence

Once agents of change have been identified, much of the best Quaker work places a strong emphasis on the cultivation of genuine partnerships with these individuals and groups. On occasion, this approach has been explicitly contrasted by our partners with the kind of hierarchical relationships that are often the norm with many international donors and supporters. Again, our relatively small size can be a real advantage here. Without vast bureaucracies behind us (such as almost inevitably emerge in larger institutions) Quakers often have the freedom to work more consistently on the basis of real relationships – on a sense of authentic solidarity born of a familiarity with the day-to-day realities of those with whom we work. I like to describe this as a ministry of presence.

The concept of a ministry of presence has a great deal to do with what one twentieth-century Quaker global witness, Roger Wilson, once described memorably as "the supremacy of divinely ordered human relations over the claims of the administrative machine" (Roger C Wilson 1953, pp31–32). It is this sense of intimacy, of an encounter between children of God based on mutual respect and trust, which is prioritised in much Quaker work. Again, this is an emphasis frequently noted by local activists who sometimes reflect bitterly on the patronising treatment they may have received from other international actors – those representatives of governments or agencies whose rare departures from their sleek, air-conditioned offices in the capital or the comforts of their shiny, white 4×4s render the conditions in which most people live and work in that society a remote and dimly understood environment.

Continuity of commitment

All global citizens today will be familiar with the way in which our sympathies with victims of armed conflict or extreme poverty can be directed or re-directed by those powerful images of suffering on which the international media decide to focus. We are well aware of the way in which an agenda for various types of intervention – whether economic, political or military – can likewise be informed or even determined by the choices of these information superpowers. This phenomenon often places enormous pressure on international nongovernmental organisations as the perceived need to demonstrate an organisation's immediate relevance to the dominant images being seen on television screens across the globe sweeps all before it. The imperatives of fundraising and the wish to secure a high public profile for the organisation's work frequently demand nothing less than significant relocations and reallocations of always over-stretched resources. As the international community lurches in this fashion from humanitarian crisis to famine to brutal civil war, the result is often a very harmful short-termism of engagement. Even though international NGOs acknowledge this to be a phenomenon that can badly distort the organisation's work or compromise its integrity, many feel they may have little choice but to follow the camera crews and packs of journalists to the next Big Disaster.

I would argue that Quakers have the ability to act as a sort of cultural resistance to this unfortunate pattern, choosing instead to place continuity of commitment at the centre of our corporate or individual interventions. Most of the fragile work for justice, peace and human rights to which Quakers are instinctively drawn in these contexts will in essence be about inherently long-term ventures. Genuine transformation takes time. At its truest, Quaker work refuses to allow a shift in media priorities, protracted difficulties with a project, or even initial failure on the ground to become a pretext for premature withdrawal. This is certainly the case with our recent work in Northern Ireland, South Asia, the Balkans and Northern Uganda. We are perhaps most ourselves as a community of faith when we make it plain to our partners that we are placing ourselves in solidarity with them for the long haul – affirming the value of alternative voices and visions even in the face of seemingly intractable local political or cultural opposition.

Quakers are certainly not exempt from the pressures of a media-led agenda for intervention. In the spring of 1999, it was the NATO intervention in Kosovo and all that followed from it that grabbed both the headlines and the hearts and minds of many British Friends. In an impassioned, specially convened Yearly Meeting session devoted to reflection on the crisis, concerned Friends launched an International Conflicts Appeal to respond to the very real spiritual demands of the hour. Friends characteristically gave generously and a large amount of money was raised in a remarkably short time. A number of fine things were made possible by those additional resources, including a series of seminars on the peace testimony for Friends around the country and support for embattled peace activists and conscientious objectors to military service in what was then the Federal Republic of Yugoslavia.

This was indisputably good work and all of it much valued by those on the receiving end. But the Appeal was very much a one-off effort generating a single, non-renewable pot of funding. And interest in the Kosovo situation – which had been very real among concerned Friends in those first months of 1999 – inevitably waned as fresh and equally compelling challenges to our peace testimony appeared elsewhere in the world. The question subsequently arose as to how Friends were to sustain those new relationships with activists in the region that had been established through this particular response, as there was no longer-term source of funding for doing so. In this instance, were Friends perhaps at risk of falling prey to the very same kind of short-termism of engagement discussed critically above? Do we not have an ethical responsibility when embarking on a new piece of Quaker work – perhaps most especially in an emergency situation – to think through how our interventions can best be sustained long after the television crews and even other nongovernmental organisations have departed the scene?

Acts of faith

Closely linked to an emphasis on continuity of commitment, much contemporary Quaker work is also rooted in a belief that our witness in the world must be understood first and foremost as an act of faith. This is to do with a deliberate focus on the processes involved in undertaking such work rather than on crude expectations of immediate results. It is the recognition that much of the work that we do or seek to support in relationship with our partners is principally seed planting, and that the fruits of these efforts may well not be seen in our own lifetimes. It is anchoring ourselves and our efforts in a sense of God's time rather than our own.

Good management is an ethical imperative for any NGO working internationally today. Sound planning and evaluation of projects in the field is undoubtedly important. Taking these management responsibilities seriously is crucial for Quakers especially if being led by the winds of the Spirit is not to deteriorate into an unfortunate tendency to be blown in all directions. But again, as a community of faith, we have the freedom to resist what too often today becomes an over-reliance on managerialism – the reduction of sometimes very tentative work to a set of "measurable objectives" or "verifiable end results".

Anyone who has worked for a large international NGO in the past decade will know how this contemporary fashion can undermine or even eliminate certain kinds of projects that by their very nature cannot be crammed into inappropriate, rigidly time-bound frameworks. Without question, we should always be seeking to instil in our partners a sense of the importance of accountability and transparency in organisational life. But Quakers are invariably going to be working in contexts where few people (particularly those imaginative, "subversive", and marginalised agents of change) have the luxury of deep personal and social security that allows us to speak confidently and precisely about what we will be doing or achieving in two or three years' time. Any approach to peacebuilding or conflict transformation that assigns value to a project or piece of work solely on the basis of some sort of predetermined "success criteria" displays little understanding of the often very delicate nature of such an enterprise.

Quaker work must always be prepared to embrace something of what Rowan Williams has described ironically as "the obstinate uselessness of witness to God's truth" (2000, p7). We must be ready for our methods and for the work of our partners to be derided by critics or cynics as "futile" or "a drop in the ocean". But we must continue to insist with an obstinacy grounded in our faith that mere utility or effectiveness is never the sole starting point for any Quaker work.

One particular story from the Bosnian context illustrates this "act of faith" foundation of Quaker work very beautifully. Several years ago, one of our former Quaker Peace & Social Witness representatives told me of a conversation she had recently had with a young Bosnian woman, a former contact she recognised from her time working in the Balkans. This young woman came from a town that had been ruthlessly "cleansed" of its Muslim population during the war. In the first years after the war, a group of local Bosnian Serbs had expressed a wish to hold a one-day meeting with a small group of willing Muslims who had lived in the town before being forcibly expelled from their

Young Bosnian Croats and Muslims, children of former enemies, co-operate on a problem-solving exercise in the Youth Centre, Gornji Vakuf/ Uskoplje, a project supported by QPSW.

homes. Having been turned down by other international donors interested only in funding large-scale projects in the region, she had come to QPSW in search of the very small sum of money that would make this experimental forum possible.

Understandably, the young woman was fearful that this risky encounter between former "enemies" could end in failure or even in open conflict. She expected that QPSW would be reluctant to offer financial support for the proposed meeting as no firm guarantee of outcome could be offered. Our representative quite rightly confounded this expectation, assuring the woman that Quakers would be eager and willing to support such a bold initiative (and even accept the prospect of outright failure) simply because of "the spiritual value of getting to the point that you are willing to try".* Several years on from this bit of seed planting, the young woman recalled with gratitude the faith which Quakers had unhesitatingly placed in this sheer gamble of an initiative. What she remembers about that initial contact is our belief in the inherent rightness of the step she and others were prepared to take, regardless of any immediate result of the encounter.

A pragmatic approach to reconciliation

Like many Friends, I have a passionate attachment to the word "reconciliation". When I hear it spoken, I jump to attention and shout "yes" instinctively. I suppose that is some sort of reflection on how internalised the peace testimony has become for me – and I expect it is much the same for most Quakers. But in our fervent wish to get to the really nice bit at the end of any story of violent conflict or a rupture in relationships, we may at times forget that peace is often a matter of darkness acknowledged and overcome rather than an absence or denial of that darkness. In our well-meaning haste, we may forget that reconciliation is a risky and at times very painful process that must happen at a pace and in a manner true to the experiences and wishes of those whom we may wish to bring together. We need to be aware of the deep damage that can be caused by premature attempts to force people to reconcile and we need to respect the intensely difficult and

---

* Conversation with Birgit Felleisen, Britain Yearly Meeting, Exeter, 1 August 2001.

often very gradual nature of this work if we are to avoid the trap of what Dietrich Bonhoeffer famously described as "cheap grace" (1963, pp45–60).

The recognition that reconciliation can rarely be served up to a divided people as an abstract concept is one of the insights into this process that has been confirmed during the extended Quaker presence in Northern Ireland and in much recent Quaker work in the Balkans. Crudely stated, to enter into any community and simply announce "We are here to reconcile you" – effectively commanding those separated by communal hatred or violence to sit down at the table, shake hands and talk it over – must always be avoided. Much recent Quaker work in this area has helped us to understand that in divided communities, reconciliation may often best be advanced through very pragmatic, small-scale initiatives (such as infrastructure reconstruction projects of common interest in war-battered towns and villages) that can open first channels of communication across that divide in a way that is safer and more effective for all those concerned. By encouraging those so minded to cross bitterly contested communal lines, not on the basis of some explicitly named "reconciliation" initiative but in order to rebuild a shared physical environment from which both "sides" will benefit, may be a far more fruitful way to begin this process than any eloquent proclamation about healing wounds and mending breaches.

This list of five qualities of Quaker global witness is by no means an exhaustive one. There are as many dimensions to Quaker international work of various kinds as there are individual Friends involved in these creative efforts. But it is my hope that this suggested framework will at the very least prove useful as a prompt for fresh thinking and discussion among British Friends about the value of Quaker global witness today. Other branches of the worldwide family of Friends will doubtless find some of the issues raised here similar if not identical to challenges faced in their own forms of global witness. Although we have chosen to focus more narrowly on British Quaker witness, everything said here could indeed be extended to include the rich experience and learning of South African Friends in their long struggle against apartheid, the work of Australian and Aotearoan/New Zealand Friends with indigenous peoples, the witness of the American Friends Service Committee and the Friends Committee on National Legislation, and countless other examples.

At the close of my Rowntree Quaker Fellowship in 2002, I was delighted to come across a couple of paragraphs in the review and evaluation of the Quaker Peace & Social Witness Northern Uganda Project which seemed to confirm much of what I had been asking local meetings to appreciate about our attempts to bring a distinctively Quaker approach to bear on contemporary peacebuilding in our violence-saturated world. Writing about the first phase of Quaker work in this long neglected part of Africa, the reviewers (all of them external to QPSW) concluded that:

> The choice of strategy makes QPSW's involvement in Gulu qualitatively different to almost any other NGO. Because QPSW has no set agenda of its own (beyond furthering peace work) it is able to stand together with local actors for peace on their own terms without any of the issues of ego or other agendas that so blight most NGOs in Northern Uganda.
>
> They have gained an understanding of the conflict and of local perceptions of the conflict that are surprising given the short period of presence (less than two years) in Gulu. The organisation and the volunteers are accepted by local people in a way that few expatriates ever win. This is testimony to three factors: the strategy chosen; the organisational ethos and values of QPSW; and the quality of the individual volunteers recruited (QPSW 2002, p2).

In today's overcrowded NGO marketplace, a progress report like that is an enviable achievement and one that should convince all of us in Britain Yearly Meeting that our Quaker global witness (however small by comparison with other agencies for good, or constrained in terms of financial resources) can be much more than a pale imitation of the large-scale programmes of the NGO giants working in this area. In choosing to bring our witness to such afflicted places as Northern Uganda, South Asia, or Bosnia, Quakers are giving vital expression to that central insight of Dietrich Bonhoeffer, who wrote in his prison cell in July 1944 that "it is only by living completely in this world that one learns to have faith . . . By this-worldliness I mean living unreservedly in life's duties, problems, successes, failures, experiences and perplexities. In so doing, we throw ourselves completely into the arms of God, taking seriously not our own sufferings, but those of God in the world . . ." (1997, pp369–370)

Chapter 2
The Prophet and the Reconciler
by Grigor McClelland

The first part of this chapter is the text of an address given in London on 28 May 1960, at the London Yearly Meeting of the Society of Friends, as an introduction to the session entitled: "Our Historic Witness in 1660 and 1960". The second and shorter part attempts to apply the same approach to some developments in the following decades.

> We utterly deny all outward wars and strife and fightings with outward weapons, for any end or under any pretence whatsoever. And this is our testimony to the whole world. The spirit of Christ, by which we are guided, is not changeable, so as once to command us from a thing as evil and again to move unto it; and we do certainly know, and so testify to the world, that the spirit of Christ, which leads us into all Truth, will never move us to fight and war against any man with outward weapons, neither for the kingdom of Christ, nor for the kingdoms of this world.

This testimony by Friends to Charles II, actually made in January 1661, but usually referred to as the 1660 declaration,* has become historic. It has given inspiration through three centuries. Why is this? Because it expresses, clearly and unmistakably, a moral insight, and recognises it for what it is. One is struck first by the glorious conviction of permanence, indeed of timelessness, in that which guided these Friends, the spirit of Christ. It is not changeable. It is eternal. Further-more, this spirit is universal, valid in all circumstances – "for any end . . . under any pretence . . . against any man". Finally, it is personal. It commands us from a thing as evil; it will never move us to fight and war. The insight is into the choice between right and wrong which faces an individual – oneself.

Today, nearly three hundred years later, we must reaffirm this classic statement of religious prophecy. We must acknowledge its

---

*See *Quaker Faith & Practice* 24.04 and 19.46; the date was affected by the 1752 calendar change.

continuing validity for ourselves who are heirs to an unbroken tradition. But we cannot honestly do so without adding to it. We have to try to answer the questions it poses for us, who live in contact with the world as well as in communion with the eternal. Its very validity and its relevance force us to try to step out over its limitations, and to discover what it implies for a different Society of Friends in a different world.

For the declaration is historical as well as historic. It is historical in the sense that it is embedded in and addressed to a particular historical situation. Friends wished (and needed) at the time of the restoration of the monarchy to reassure the new king that they would not take up arms against him. Partly as a result, the statement is negative. It says nothing of reconciliation. It makes no mention of inward fighting or spiritual struggle. It does not tell us whether and how evil may be overcome without outward weapons. It is confined to personal conscientious objection, whilst the world today challenges us to creative Christian pacifism and peacemaking.

If we say in 1960 that we cannot fight and war with outward weapons, we are asked two supplementary questions. First, if it is wrong for us to use outward weapons, is it not also wrong for all men and nations? And if so, is it not our duty to seek to convince them of this? Secondly, if conditions are such that nations, beset by fear, cannot bring themselves to accept this truth, is there not an obligation on us to seek to alter these conditions and to remove this fear?

These two questions encapsulate two approaches to world peace which are contending amongst us. I can best illustrate these approaches by telling you about two friends of mine, whom I shall call the prophet and the reconciler. Both are essentially Quakers: their attitudes and actions are based on inward spiritual experience which carries its own authority and compulsion. Both are personal pacifists, in the sense that they have experienced the validity of the 1660 declaration for themselves, and conscientiously object to bearing outward weapons. Both are of course sinners, and (what is more) acutely conscious of their inadequacies.

But the prophet devotes herself to preaching the unilateral abandonment of arms as a moral duty. She is engaged on a crusade to bring to her fellow human beings a consciousness that war is wrong.

She calls them, whether as humble citizens or as national leaders, to cast away all arms, come what may.

The reconciler, on the other hand, devotes himself to working for the establishment of conditions in which people will feel no need to rely on arms because they do not feel threatened. He seeks to relax tensions, to promote meetings of persons and meetings of minds, to suggest acceptable solutions for divisive problems.

Each of these two has considered the role of the other, and is critical of it. The prophet thinks the reconciler is compromising truth. The reconciler thinks the prophet is being unrealistic.

Both are present in this room. I don't suggest that they are here as separate individuals. They exist in me, and in the heart of each one of us. A perpetual dialogue is going on between them, in all our hearts. Now one, now the other, gets the upper hand; now one, now the other, is on the defensive. Let us listen, in a little more detail, to this dialogue.

We find the prophet, not only seeking to bring other individuals to the point of sharing, as a personal moral conviction, valid for themselves, the deep conscientious objection she feels to taking human life whatever the circumstances, but also advocating what she calls positive Christian pacifism; that is, the expression in national policy as well as in personal sentiment of a spirit of Christian love for the whole of mankind, with all that that implies. The crux of such a policy, in her view, is not mere willingness to compromise, or a new spirit in negotiations, or even a massive programme of material aid to poor countries. It is a nation adopting a course of complete and unilateral disarmament and saying to the potential aggressor and oppressor: "We will let you overrun our country rather than use outward weapons to stop you. We will not protect ourselves – or others – from you by arms because we love your citizens, as children of God, too much to try to destroy them. We will struggle – nonviolently – against the evil you do, but whatever you do to us, we will still love you."

But the reconciler objects. He says to the prophet: "This policy demands a readiness to go to the Cross. Do you make that clear? It could, if adopted by Britain, ignite the holocaust of a Third (and Final) World War. Have you faced the grave responsibility you take upon yourself? It would compel a sacrifice from many who are not ready to offer it. Ought you not rather to be saying to them: 'Wear thy sword as long as thou canst'?"

The prophet accepts the charge of irresponsibility by passing the buck, in effect, to God. She feels called, not to take heed for consequences but to preach righteousness. As a matter of practical assessment, she may well calculate that a national policy expressing a spirit of Christian love for all mankind is the only sane policy, but she does not rely on calculation. In the last resort she falls back on faith – the faith that by such a possibly sacrificial act, and only by such an act, God's power is released into this world, to work a transformation in his own way and in his own good time.

What now of the reconciler? "Blessed are the peacemakers, for they shall be called the children of God" (Matthew 5:9). His heart is torn by the thought of man's estrangement from man, no less than the prophet's is by man's estrangement from God. He feels laid upon him the ministry of reconciliation between individuals and between groups. But he sees divisions and enmities as infinitely complex situations to which there is no single or simple solution. He accepts the apparent limitations of the minds of those who are divided, and tries to work within these limitations. He tries to reassure and to suggest actions which will provide reassurance; he tries to wean gently from pathological attitudes. To act therapeutically in this way, to exercise this almost pastoral vocation, he must not impose his own solutions, he must not always have his own axe to grind. He must be acceptable.

"For the sake of being acceptable," argues the prophet, "you water down the Gospel. You soft-pedal the Truth. You are afraid that if you let them know what you really think, they will laugh at you and you will lose what influence you may have. In the end – if it hasn't happened already – you will become corrupted and lose your faith and it will be left to others to carry it on.

"Moreover," she adds, "every time you suggest a compromise you betray your principles. How can you work to save the nuclear non-proliferation treaty when it accepts retention of nuclear weapons by existing nuclear powers for years to come? How can you commend a United Nations peacekeeping force when you would not be prepared to carry a rifle yourself?"

The reconciler replies that half a loaf is better than no bread, that

Young Catholic and English volunteers who took part in a Quaker playscheme for children in Northern Ireland, 1991, with a Protestant police officer.

Quakers at the Iraq war demonstration, 15 February 2003.

people can establish trustful relations without being pacifists, that particular small concessions, despite their being unaccompanied by any complete lowering of the guard, may nevertheless stimulate reciprocal concessions and start off a chain reaction in the direction of peace. Furthermore, that conversion is often not an instantaneously complete process, and that you have to take people as you find them, working on the material before you in the situation in which you are, supporting a little here, strengthening a little there, elsewhere removing a simple misunderstanding or attacking some clearly irrational fear.

And so the dialogue goes on, within (I believe) each one of us who is sensitive both to the demands of the Spirit and to the conditions of the world.

The above was written in 1960 and I then illustrated the difference between the two positions by their likely reactions to the breakdown in May 1960 of a "summit" meeting between Dwight Eisenhower, then president of the USA, and Nikita Khrushchev, then general secretary of the USSR, caused by the grounding of an American spy plane, the U2, over Soviet territory. I suggested that the reconciler would be looking at the role of fear in the situation and asking how to repair the breach in the delicate structure of mutual confidence; while the prophet would be arguing that you cannot create the conditions of peace while seeking at the same time to ensure your military security – negotiations between two sides armed to the teeth are almost bound to break down.

It is obvious that in the half century since then the world has changed vastly. We therefore need to examine the positions of the prophet and the reconciler today. The Cold War has ended, and we have moved from a bi-polar to a uni-polar world with the USA as the sole superpower. The world is more populous, richer, more unequal, economically and culturally more integrated (into a "global village") and more dangerous. Climate change has emerged as a new common problem facing humanity. The devastating attack on the Twin Towers in New York of 11 September 2001 began a new period of international terrorism and measures designed to frustrate and uproot it. Events in the Balkans, Africa and elsewhere, with genocide or "ethnic cleansing" and "failed states", have led to new doctrines of intervention by foreign powers in sovereign countries to protect human rights.

The reconciler now can point to some significant successes in building world order by negotiation, such as international conventions on chemical and bacteriological weapons, the establishment of an international court of justice, and the Kyoto treaty on climate change. The prophet can point to the remarkable unilateral measures of disarmament and withdrawal by the Soviet Union under Mikhail Gorbachev, and the role of people power in the "velvet" revolutions of Eastern Europe.

Two major changes are of special interest in our context. In South Africa, apartheid was ended and democracy established, through a combination of a widespread prophetic commitment to justice inside that country and in the wider world, and through negotiations between reconciliatory individuals in the respective leaderships, with some crucial assistance by third parties. And afterwards, a pioneering Truth and Reconciliation Commission helped the perpetrators and victims of injustice to work through their experiences and reach mutual understanding and even forgiveness.

A second major peaceful change occurred in the southern states of the USA, of which only early stages were visible in 1960. There were occasions of mass nonviolent confrontation standing for equality and justice in prophetic tones. There were also initiatives to bring together the oppressors and the oppressed. American Quakers as prophets supported the marchers, the bus boycotters and the freedom riders, and as reconcilers worked with those who discriminated in employment, education and real estate.

In much smaller contexts, also, both approaches have been manifested. Friends are practising reconciliation in relation to partnerships (Relate), families, neighbours and communities (community mediation), crime (restorative justice), sexual offenders (Circles of Support and Accountability), denominational and political allegiance (Quaker House, Belfast), and tribal and ethnic conflict (Responding to Conflict). Friends have also taken part in prophetic protest at Greenham Common, Holy Loch, and Menwith Hill; they have marched in opposition to the invasion of Iraq, and refused to pay the portion of their taxes attributable to arms. The two sorts of witness are complementary.

A new and distinctive witness is that of "accompaniment", as practised in particular in the Israeli-occupied territories of Palestine. Accompaniers, from the Society and other churches, accompany Palestinians passing through checkpoints, children going to school, families whose dwellings are being destroyed. They are exposed to potential violence but their distinctive identification gives them a measure of protection. Their presence indicates to the occupying personnel that their actions are being independently observed. They thus portray the values of the outside world. At the same time they make possible dialogue with the occupiers. Prophecy and reconciliation thus merge.

At the level of global conflict, however, we have hardly begun. The East-West polarity of the 1950s and after, when Friends attempted to play some role, has been replaced by Al-Qaeda on the one hand and on the other the evangelical Christian and neo-conservative interests behind the administration in Washington. Each of these has intractable and entrenched positions and a visceral fear and hatred of the other. Can our peace testimony lead us as reconcilers to promote any mutual understanding between these two, or as prophets to speak truth to the power they represent?

Chapter 3
Quaker Concern
by Diana & John Lampen

"Concern" in the Quaker sense is defined by Roger Wilson, the 1949 Swarthmore lecturer: "The individual . . . knows, as a matter of inward experience, that there is something that the Lord would have done, however obscure the way, however uncertain the means to human observation" (Roger C Wilson 1949, p12).* This is not a purely Quaker phenomenon; it is common in the Bible and the histories of most faiths, and perhaps does not even need a religious context.†

This experience seems to develop in one of two ways. Some people become obsessed with a set of problems which seems to offer no way forward. Feelings of anxiety, compassion, and hopelessness go round and round in the mind; and then suddenly, without conscious effort, the treadmill stops, and a possible course of action (or at least a first step) presents itself accompanied with a feeling of calm and certainty. The American Quaker John Woolman is best known today for his witness against slavery. In 1742 his master asked him to draw up a bill of sale for a slave; he did so, but it threw him into turmoil until a similar request a few months later gave him the opportunity to refuse, taking the first step in what became a lifelong concern. It has often happened to someone engaged in organised Quaker work, that a specific concern has emerged from the welter of their activities and encounters, as subsequent chapters of this book will show.

In the other form, the impetus comes "out of the blue" – though a vague and unspecific unease may have grown in the person over time, like that which some people sense before an earthquake without knowing why. It can be a sense of dissatisfaction with one's life, or a feeling that one is looking for something without knowing what. Then suddenly something happens urging one towards an action which one had never thought of taking. An 18-year-old Colombian geophysics

---

* Also at *Quaker Faith & Practice* 13.07.

† See many of the stories in *European Centre for Conflict Prevention: People Making Peace II*.

student, Jaime Jaramillo, saw a street girl killed by a lorry as she ran out to pick up a cigarette box off the street which turned out to be empty. "At that moment," he said, "I discovered what I was born to do." He took up a career in the oil industry in order to fund his ceaseless efforts to befriend and rescue the lost children of the city sewers.

There are many ways in which the prompting can come. It can be a chance encounter or a sudden coincidence which is felt to contain a message. A call can come in the form of a "voice" or a dream. James Nayler said in 1652, "I was at the plough, meditating on the things of God, and suddenly I heard a voice saying to me, 'Get thee out from thy kindred and from thy father's house'. And I had a promise given with it, whereupon I did exceedingly rejoice that I had heard the voice of that God which I had professed from a child, but never known him" (1716, p12).* Paul of Tarsus, preaching in Asia Minor, dreamed of a man in Greek dress saying, "Come over into Macedonia and help us" (Acts 16:9). Sometimes we are inspired by a message, intended or accidental, from someone else. In our own case, John went to live in Northern Ireland and work there for peace in 1983. When Diana came to join him a year later she was feeling uncertain and worried about her own role. She was invited to visit a largely Roman Catholic prayer group, at which a man said, "I have a message for someone, but I don't know for whom. God says to you, 'Don't worry about what you're to do; I will bring to you one by one the people I want you to care for.'" And that is what happened; she learnt to live in trust. Of course a concern may be the outcome of a logical train of thought, but Roger Wilson says, "Often proposals for action are made which have every appearance of good sense, but as the [Quaker] meeting waits before God, it becomes clear that the proposition falls short of 'concern'."

As we ourselves became gripped by concerns which we then took up, we were never given a full plan of action, only a first step. We took comfort from John Woolman who wrote, "I have sometimes felt a necessity to stand up, but that spirit which is of the world hath prevailed in so many, and the pure life of truth been so pressed down, that I have gone forward not as one travelling in a road cast up and well prepared, but as a man walking through a miry place wherein are stones here and there, safe to step on but so situated that, one step

---

* Also at *Quaker Faith & Practice* 19.09.

being taken, time is necessary to see where to step next" (1774, p243).*
This was certainly true of him. Four years after he refused to write the
instrument of slavery, a visit to Carolina brought him face to face with
large-scale slavery. He then wrote *Some Considerations on the Keeping
of Negroes*, apparently to clarify his own thinking, because he did not
submit the manuscript to his Yearly Meeting until 1754, four years after
his dying father told him that he should (Jean Solerland 2003, pp151–
154). That was the start of his struggle to convince Philadelphia Friends
that slave owning was against Christian principles.

When Stephen Grellet, a Friend visiting from America, invited
Elizabeth Fry to go into Newgate Prison in 1813 she just gave out
armfuls of baby clothes and spoke to a few women (June Rose 1994,
p70). It was four years before she returned to begin what was to
become her life's work in prison education and reform. Will Warren
was a 65-year-old English Quaker who felt led to go and live in one
of the most violent areas of Northern Ireland in 1971. He said to us,
"The Holy Spirit doesn't give you very much briefing . . . I only knew
that I had been sent to listen, to listen to people on both sides; and
maybe, one day, to help them to listen to one another" (John Lampen
1983, p5). His work in Londonderry developed through unforeseen
events and chance encounters, to which he brought a talent for
making friendships. In the end he was trusted by Roman Catholic
and Protestant clergy, police, paramilitary gunmen on both sides,
community workers, politicians and government officials, members of
reconciliation groups and countless ordinary people in need of help.
Many children who knew him have told us how it was Will's inspiration
which, years later, prevented them from joining an armed group.

Typically the concern, as it turns into action, is shaped by
unexpected encounters. There is an interesting observation by Goethe,
which we can testify is true to our own experience: "Until one is
committed, there is hesitancy, the chance to draw back, continuous
ineffectiveness, concerning all acts of initiative and creation. There
is one elementary truth, the ignorance of which kills countless ideas
and splendid plans: that the moment one definitely commits oneself,
Providence moves too. All sorts of things occur to help one that would
never otherwise have occurred. A whole stream of events issues from

---

* This passage is omitted from Phillips Moulton's edition.

that decision, favouring one with many kinds of unforeseen incidents, meetings and material assistance which no one could have dreamed would come his way."*

The Old Testament contains many instances of God commanding a prophet to do some irrational action, like burying a linen cloth in the ground. This was the early Quaker model for their own experiences of being led by God to some task. Clearly the ideas of "success" and "failure" do not apply to such actions. The criterion is obedience, and when the task is fully performed, the doer feels "clear" of it, even though there are no visible results. George Fox noted, "Having stayed some time in London . . . and cleared myself of what services the Lord had at that time laid upon me there, I passed out of London into Kent . . . "(George Fox 1975, p285). John Woolman provides another instructive example. As a culmination of his campaign against slavery, he felt that perhaps he was being called to visit the West Indies. But "in the Quarterly and General Spring Meetings I found no clearness to express anything further than that I believed resignation herein was required of me. Having obtained certificates from all the said meetings I felt like a sojourner at my outward habitation and kept free from worldly encumbrances" (John Woolman 1989, p158). Not long after, he heard of a Quaker-owned ship about to sail from Philadelphia; but when invited to go and see the vessel, "I had not clearness in my mind to go but I went to my lodging . . . I was for a time as one who knew not what to do, and was tossed in a [spiritual] tempest . . . Having been two days in town, I believed my obedience to my Heavenly Father consisted in returning homeward . . ."

Modern Quakers too have testified that action under concern is not to be justified by apparent results. George Lakey, a contemporary American Quaker peace activist, described to us how he went to give a training in Thailand to student exiles from Burma. After the first day he felt that there were too many obstacles; with cultural differences, different expectations, varying experiences in the group, jet lag and the hot climate, he was failing to communicate. He felt angry and frustrated. Then he told himself, "Remember that you are in the East, which gave humankind the message of non-attachment. Why am I so attached to notions of success and failure? My only task here is to be

---

* We would be grateful to anyone who can trace this quotation for us.

true to my own skills, knowledge and spirit. The rest is not and was never in my hands."* He then felt at peace in himself and the work went much better.

Personal and group discernment

In the very beginnings of our Society, such leadings were enough to prompt a Friend into action; if one felt the divine call, it seemed that no human permission was needed. Mary Fisher was a servant girl who became a Friend and suffered severe punishment for it in England and New England. But "she would not be at rest till she went in person to the Great Emperor of the Turks and informed him concerning the Errors of his religion and the Truth of hers" (William Sewel 1722, p294). There was no formal process at the time to test her concern, but the group at Swarthmoor Hall gave her a little money and she set out with four Friends in 1657. Losing her companions one by one, she seems to have walked for five hundred miles across Greece alone, till she reached the imperial army base at Adrianople (Edirne) and amazingly obtained an audience with the brutal Ottoman sultan where she gave her message and returned safely home.

But after two Friends, James Nayler and John Perrot, had brought the whole Quaker community into some danger and division by individual activity, it was recognised that a person might misperceive a call or "outrun his Guide". Some checks and balances were needed. In 1662 Edward Burrough urged the setting up of a weekly meeting in London, separate from the group of travelling ministers who preached there; he said this would be valuable "in advising and consenting unto one another, in what we are each of us called to manage and perform on the Lord's behalf, for his service: not acting for self-ends, apart, reservedly, or oppositely one to another, in any work pretendedly for the Lord; but going on in unity together, asking, giving and taking counsel, advice and information one of another in the Lord; and all for the better carrying on his good work, that it may prosper in the earth" (A R Barclay 1841, p301).

This is the origin of the procedure prescribed in *Quaker Faith & Practice*: "As a general rule concerns should be brought before a preparative or, where appropriate, monthly meeting. The concern

---

* Personal communication.

may, if recognised by that meeting as a true leading, then be forwarded to other meetings for consideration by a wider or more specialised group of Friends" (13.06). The prime task of the meeting should be to discern whether this is "a religiously valid concern". It may then offer support – financial, practical or spiritual – or adopt it as a concern of the whole meeting. Thus Swansea Meeting (with the encouragement of South Wales Monthly Meeting) supported the Quaker church in Madagascar, following a visit to them by some of its members (Barbara Prys-Williams 1996). We will call this the "traditional process". This procedure is under some strain today for a number of reasons which arise out of our history.

In the eighteenth and nineteenth centuries the great majority of leadings which were brought to Friends meetings were to "travel in the ministry", that is to take the Christian Quaker message either to make new converts or to strengthen isolated Quaker groups. The task was a familiar one, so the members of the home meeting had only to decide whether this individual was truly called and adequate to the task. If so, a "travelling minute" or certificate was issued which prevented fraudulent claims of membership (since the minister would be given free hospitality) and certified the meeting's recognition of her or his gifts of teaching. Ministers usually travelled in pairs, so it was common to send untried ones with more experienced Friends whose task might be not to speak but to support and guide their colleagues. We may take Isaac Sharp as an example of the minuting process; in 1877 at the age of 71 he asked Darlington Monthly Meeting to release him for a journey around the world, including South Africa, Australia, New Zealand and California. "For the space of half an hour, amid a deep and very solemn stillness, he was engaged in unfolding the burden of many years – startling in its successive stages and almost overwhelming in its effects; he was graciously helped and sustained, without faltering, to the end and then calmly and quietly sat down" (J Ormerod Greenwood 1977, p156). The meeting issued a travelling certificate, which was endorsed by Meeting for Sufferings.

But there could be tensions between the individual and the meetings which authorised or received them. When John Woolman arrived at London Yearly Meeting with a certificate from his yearly meeting, he was dressed in undyed cloth and dishevelled from having

Isaac Sharp

come straight from the ship after an arduous journey. Some Friends took fright at his appearance, thinking he might be "an itinerant enthusiast". (We may not use the phrase now, but we know just what they meant!) One of them suggested that, having come to the Yearly Meeting, he might feel he had discharged his concern and could go straight home (Henry Cadbury 1971, p45). Isaac Sharp too could cause problems. On his 86th birthday he was lying ill in California after an arduous journey through South Africa, India and Japan. When they heard that his life was despaired of, Meeting for Sufferings in London panicked and withdrew his certificate; but by then the old man, "driven by a dæmon" as Ormerod Greenwood says, was halfway to China to undertake the task he felt called to – a dangerous 1500-mile journey up the Yangtse River (J Ormerod Greenwood 1977, p155). It is helpful to recall William Braithwaite's warning: "It is with individuals rather than communities that new truth originates . . . While corporate guidance is of great value in controlling extravagances, it is a source of great danger to the church if it is opposed to a genuine individual concern" (1909, p101).*

These procedures did not preclude Friends from acting alone, particularly on matters of social concern which for two centuries were hardly ever adopted by British yearly or monthly meetings (the campaign against slavery being a conspicuous exception). Richard Reynolds the eighteenth-century Quaker ironmaster even practised his philanthropy under pseudonyms as he believed Christ had commanded (Arthur Raistrick 1968, p145).† Friends did not need to get Quaker permission to work with other bodies. Samuel Gurney the nineteenth-century Quaker MP was deeply engaged in a great deal of "concerned" work, including three hospitals, the YMCA, the Aborigines Protection Society and the RSPCA; but all of these were interdenominational bodies, and he did not seek formal Quaker approval. When so-called "self-appointed bodies" began to appear among British Friends in the 1850s, they encountered a good deal of Quakerly resistance to what was called "creaturely activity" – in contrast to the work of spreading the Quaker gospel. Even such an innocent activity as preparing Sunday School materials was opposed on the grounds that children should be trained to sit through the silent meeting and wait on the promptings of the Holy Spirit. One Friend of the time wrote: "Meetings for discipline . . . were almost entirely in the hands of those of middle and advanced life, and repression rather than encouragement of spiritual effort was the order of the day" (Charles Linney, quoted in J Ormerod Greenwood 1977, p208). It is no wonder that special groups were formed to pursue concerns which did not have the sanction of the Society as a whole. Towards the end of the nineteenth century there was a more general reaction which led gradually to the modern London (now Britain) Yearly Meeting, with its departments specifically entrusted with Quaker concerns for what was once condemned as "creaturely activity".

From "leading" to action

It is of course perfectly proper to carry out small-scale concerns requiring personal action without formal reference to anyone else.

---

* Also quoted in *Quaker Faith & Practice* 13.10.
† His biblical inspiration was Matthew 6:1 4.

In what follows we are considering leadings which spring from widely held Quaker principles, which touch on national or international issues, and which might potentially be adopted by the whole yearly meeting. The twentieth-century Friend was given four ways of putting these into action. One was to take the concern through the traditional process, hoping that it might be seen as "Quaker work" and supported – perhaps even performed – by the local meeting or an appropriate yearly meeting department. Work taken up in this way forms the subject of other chapters in this book. The second one was to set up a "self-appointed body" (nowadays called a "Listed Informal Group") consisting of Friends willing to commit themselves to this particular cause. Thirdly one might join or create an undenominational or even nonreligious organisation specifically devoted to the task: Save the Children, Oxfam and Amnesty International are among the bodies which had Friends deeply involved in their beginnings. The fourth option was simply to get to work, trusting that the original leading was valid and should be followed – and believing, like Goethe, that unexpected help would be given. We know some concerned Friends who have set up their own small support groups; and this option may include an appeal to a Quaker Trust, which is often better placed to give funds than the yearly meeting and practises its own process of discernment – however, it does not give continuing supervision.

Most of our Listed Informal Groups consist of Friends widely spread among our meetings but linked by a common interest, such as vegetarianism or Esperanto. There is sometimes controversy over whether they should call themselves "Quaker" since there has been no endorsement by the Yearly Meeting, but they justify the name because their common interest arises out of their Quaker beliefs. Sometimes the programme is specific and the aim is to persuade other Friends to adopt it, as with the Quaker Land Value Group, and Quaker Concern for Animals. They have the advantages of easy access to Quaker magazines to express their views, a presence at Quaker gatherings, and a small management structure which is independent and hopefully like-minded.

When a concern is likely to appeal to a range of people from different backgrounds, non-Quaker organisations are often the best way forward, witnessing to the fact that people of goodwill can work together even though their beliefs may be very different. Charles Carter noted that there can be a dangerous illusion of Quaker uniqueness. Reviewing Roger Wilson's *Quaker Relief 1940–1948* in *The Friend* he wrote: "What was this 'concern' which grew so fast under the pressure of war . . . and died away so quickly afterwards? Many of us have slowly been discovering, in the post-war years, that much of the service which we thought so unique and so valuable was being done on a larger scale by others, more quietly, more efficiently, as part of their simple duty. It may be that Quakerism will not regain its effectiveness until we have learned to be ashamed of the proud myth of our uniqueness – and have learned to do our duty quietly and well, unsustained by thoughts of our own great significance" (Charles C Carter 1952).

But there are many concerns which should be taken through the traditional Quaker process. There are two reasons for this. One is that the vitality of our Society depends (among other things) on the recognition and adoption of new God-given concerns; otherwise Quaker work gradually becomes routine and uninspired. The other is that certain concerns can only be rightly judged by being submitted to our peculiar processes of discernment. Any ensuing action can properly be called "Quaker work".

But an individual Friend's attempt to do this (even when backed by his or her local meeting) can lead to the sense of strain which we mentioned. There have been significant changes in the world of philanthropic work since Friends first employed the Quaker discernment process. Work with people in need – such as war victims, AIDS sufferers, unschooled children or starving communities – is no longer a task for well-meaning amateurs. A number of British Friends felt concerns to come on short visits to Northern Ireland during the years of violence, often with ready-made peace proposals (one enthusiast suggested bringing 100, or even 1000, peace-loving Friends with him!). The more specific the suggestions, the more reluctant Irish Friends felt about welcoming such visitors; while British meetings tended to encourage their members in anything which might conceivably help the cause of peace. A realistic screening process was needed which could distinguish between the inspired idea and the eccentric one, between the suitable worker and the over-confident one.

In the second half of the last century Quaker Peace & Service (QPS), a department of Britain Yearly Meeting, often provided this. In 1998 John felt a clear leading to return to Uganda. He had worked there in 1986 and 1988 for QPS, to develop peace education after twenty years of civil war. While there he had helped in the formation of the Ugandan Fellowship of Reconciliation (JYAK). QPS recognised his renewed concern and met the costs of the visit, leaving the planning and arrangements entirely to him. JYAK took him to Western Uganda, where he joined their local trainers in work which eventually led to the founding of a dynamic grassroots anti-landmine network. QPS paid the airfare for a subsequent visit, sending a staff member with him.

But it was becoming increasingly clear that Quaker Peace & Service was stretching its resources too widely, at a time when the funds available to it were getting smaller. Its World Regional Programme Committee did not want to lose touch with the expertise of those Friends who had an intimate knowledge of peace and development issues in many parts of the world; so it set up Interest Groups for Africa, Central and Eastern Europe, the Middle East and other areas where it had been active. While noting that funds for the expansion of work were limited, the Committee expressed the hope of two-way communication in which these groups could bring "any matters considered of importance" to its notice and it could explain its policy to them (QPS 1999).

Then in 2002 Quaker Peace & Service (mainly concerned with overseas issues) and Quaker Social Responsibility & Education (working within Great Britain) were combined into a new department called Quaker Peace & Social Witness (QPSW). Practical considerations of funding and workload demanded a change of approach. It would have been impossible to provide all the different types of support Friends acting under concern might need, and the decision had to be taken to focus on a smaller number of defined projects. QPSW was still guided by Friends' current concerns. These were mostly expressed through its own managed work, developed with its great knowledge and excellent contacts in the field. It was no longer possible to offer financial support to John's anti-landmine work, though the QPSW Projects Manager for Africa, Martin Wilkinson, continued to take a close interest in it and kept John in touch with QPSW's own project in Northern Uganda.

Diana and John Lampen meeting landmine survivors in Uganda.

This policy change brought some clear benefits. Instead of coming under frequent pressure to undertake new and unrelated concerns, the department was able to provide long-term programmes offering the continuity of concern described in Chapter 1 by Brian Phillips. These are developed over time and managed by experienced committees. The new pattern was in tune with the development of professionalism over the last 25 years among nongovernmental organisations (NGOs) working in aid, relief, development and peacebuilding. The days of the inspired amateur are over; workers are expected to be informed, trained and focussed, and a range of management procedures have been learnt from the business world to ensure that they are. Before any venture is undertaken, most NGOs demand a "proposal" containing informed analysis of the context, clear aims and specific objectives, detailed strategies and a list of indicators to show if objectives are being reached. Moreover, important changes in employment law have defined new responsibilities which require a clearer line of management from every agency towards those working on its behalf.

This is a welcome reaction to the fuzzy thinking that if you go somewhere with good intentions, you will probably do some good, even if you don't know quite what it is. (Ormerod Greenwood's *Friends and Relief* contains many stories of astonishing achievement, but just as many of failures, misunderstandings, disagreements, misplaced efforts, and "just muddling through", despite the sincerity and concern of those undertaking them who believed they were following the Light.) Brian Phillips suggests that today we must identify those best placed to make a difference: thus in work in former Yugoslavia, the Quaker element is provided by committee and QPSW staff, while the actual workers are Serbs, Croats and Bosniaks who are in tune with Quaker values and also have strong local experience and credibility.

Corporate acknowledgement of what Friends are doing

However beneficial a change is, there are bound to be some regrets and questions. We would like to focus on three of these, and suggest ways to ensure that important values from the past are not lost. These are (a) the risk of conflicts between discernment and management processes within a Quaker department; (b) the question of how Britain Yearly Meeting can give equal respect to the international work of any of its members; and (c) how groups and individuals under concern can get the benefit of discernment and support from other Friends.

(a) The potential conflict between the non-rational process of Quaker discernment and the demands of informed efficient management is not new. It was explored for an earlier generation in Roger Wilson's Swarthmore Lecture, drawing on his experience as General Secretary of Friends Relief Service from 1940 to 1946. Ideally, he says, "organisation, provided it is neither top-heavy nor an end in itself, is the greatest liberator of the spirit." But he also points out, "In relief work the people in the field are continually meeting the unprecedented; and they often feel, quite truly, that their responsibility for meeting a need must take precedence over general administrative tidiness . . ." (Roger C Wilson 1949, pp42 43). Brian Phillips' discussion of acts of faith on page 19 of this book points to the same tension. It can be difficult to square the usual NGO demand for clear initial objectives and indicators with the Quaker idea of a process which unfolds gradually with a great deal of listening, waiting and responding intuitively to events – and which is completed only when one feels "clear", not when success or failure is obvious. Brian gives a striking description of how QPSW listened for half a year in Bosnia, often to unknown people, in order to discern what if anything the department should do there. He urges us to recognise that much Quaker global witness is seed planting, whose results are not susceptible to conventional evaluation and may not be measurable in our lifetime.

Will Warren's work provides an example of an act of faith having unpredictable results. After three years in Derry he negotiated an agreement between the paramilitaries there that neither side would commit sectarian murders, an agreement which held almost unbroken for twenty years. There was no way that this extraordinary achievement could have been anticipated in a list of objectives and indicators. His whole mission can only be evaluated in terms of the concept of "clearness" which we described earlier, not by any measurable results. He felt he had not achieved much, writing, "I cannot be complacent about my record in Derry. So much I saw needed doing and so much I did not do" (John Lampen 1983, p46). But the consequences of his work were still reverberating when we lived there years afterwards. The Ugandan anti-landmines network which we have described grew out of a chain of events which most people would call coincidences. Potential funders might shake their heads at these ways of proceeding; but Quaker truthfulness does not allow us to tailor funding applications to suit the preferences of possible donors, which is a constant temptation to non-Quaker groups with whom we have worked.

British Friends' central work is not dominated by modern management processes, and (as Brian explains) this distinguishes Friends from most other humanitarian bodies. But QPSW staff have told us that they feel pressures in that direction. If we were to shut the door on discernment processes which cannot be fully explained in rational terms, we would lose part of the Quaker understanding of concern. It was those processes which set in motion the witness cited earlier of John Woolman, Elizabeth Fry, Isaac Sharp, Will Warren and the others.

(b) We said earlier that when a concern for a global problem moves through proper Quaker discernment processes into action, it can rightly be called "Quaker work". This does not give a guarantee that the vision will not subsequently be lost or muddled (and we will suggest below how this may be avoided). But it does imply that the work becomes part of Britain Yearly Meeting's witness to the world. In our own time in Derry, we and the Quaker representatives in Quaker House Belfast saw each other as equal partners needing one another's support; it made no difference that theirs was a project of QPS and Ireland Yearly Meeting and ours was not. But when we have worked overseas, our local partner organisations – especially if they have had previous contact with Friends – often wanted to know if ours is an official Quaker involvement or whether we were "acting on our own". In dealing with a bureaucracy, for instance in the former Soviet Union, that can be a crucial question. In the days when QPS supported personal initiatives, it was possible to say, "Yes, our Society endorses this work".

How far should British Friends claim ownership of work which our formal organisation does not manage? This is not a question of money. We believe that if a concern is rightly discerned, the means to follow it will come – but not necessarily through an official Quaker body. Will Warren only received occasional support from QPS funds alongside many other unsystematic donations; but he had a close relationship with QPS staff, who saw him as a key part of Friends' response to the Northern Ireland situation in the 1970s (John Lampen 1983, p44). In John's anti-landmine work in Uganda, the grants which John received from QPS were extremely welcome but they were not essential. When the decision was made not to support John's visits after 2001, the costs were met (often unexpectedly) from other sources.

A related question is how to inform British Friends about remarkable personal initiatives like Roswitha Jarman's ongoing peacebuilding in the Northern Caucasus, one of a tiny handful of Quaker-led projects in the former Soviet Union. It is not that such Friends are seeking recognition for their own sake, and many of them are shy of anything which looks like self-advertisement. But much of this work is inspiring and prophetic, and it would benefit everyone if it was recorded and indeed celebrated by the Yearly Meeting as an integral part of its contribution in the world. One of the most inspiring parts of the annual QPSW conference can be the session when many Friends are given a short time to speak about projects they have initiated themselves.

It seems to us that there could be a better connection between the Quaker work managed by the Yearly Meeting through its departments and that undertaken by other Friends. In QPSW's aims, listed in 2003, we find: "We see QPSW as the hub for linking the activities of Friends which take Quaker testimonies into action . . . We will engage with groups, including Friends' meetings and other Quaker and non-Quaker groups in Britain and across the world, to support them and learn from them in whatever way we can." This was too big a dream to be achieved easily; but it is not forgotten, as QPSW's new database of local witness and projects shows. Many of the smaller ventures (such as Theresa and Ronald Watts' concern for AIDS victims in Southern Africa) are represented in the Special Interest Groups set up by QPS; but these have lost their original linkage to a central department and are now among our Listed Informal Groups. The RECAST proposals * which are before Yearly Meeting as we write recognise this in saying, "We have considered how best to value [the listed informal groups] and whether the yearly meeting needs a better defined relationship with them. There is minimal communication and accountability between them and our formal structures; we have asked whether contacts could usefully be increased for the benefit of all." The proposals recommend that these groups "are invited to conferences and to joint meetings with relevant bodies where appropriate" (this has happened); "their work is included from time to time in *Quaker News*; they are given publicity through being linked to the Britain Yearly Meeting website; the criteria for listing them are reviewed." All of these ideas seem to us helpful.

British Friends should also consider revitalising our traditional "ladder of discernment". Many monthly meetings send general concerns to Meeting for Sufferings in the hope that they may be taken up by the central departments; but it is much rarer for a Friend

---

* RECAST stands for The Working Group on Representation, Communication and Accountability in Our Structures. Its proposals were considered at Britain Yearly Meeting 2005, but final decisions will be made in 2006 or later.

to come there with a minute from his or her monthly meeting for endorsement, as Lucy Behenna did in 1980 when she created Mothers for Peace. A problem here is that local Friends may be very willing to commend the spiritual integrity of one of their members; but they often lack the expertise to evaluate whether the Friend has the necessary skills and whether the work is actually needed, practical, unlikely to do harm, and wanted by the recipients. When a local meeting decides it cannot evaluate a leading properly, it is advisable to refer the matter onwards, though *Quaker Faith & Practice* warns against doing this too readily (13.06). QPSW is very willing to advise Friends who are considering personal and small group initiatives in global witness. Indeed a minute of Meeting for Sufferings in 2002 advises, "It is essential that before forwarding a concern the monthly meeting should consult at an early stage with the relevant standing committee or department in order to find out what facts and experience can be offered to its consideration of a concern." This might well include information that the concern in question is already being addressed, perhaps by American Friends Service Committee or one of the Quaker United Nations Offices.

Where the monthly meeting does unite with an individual's concern and feels it has a wide significance, there is nothing (except perhaps pressure of business) to stop us reviving and adapting the "certificate", a document endorsed by the local and yearly meetings which released a Friend for service.* This is a tradition going back long before Isaac Sharp into the early eighteenth century. Given the professionalism now expected in humanitarian work, this could provide a channel for QPSW's advice and oversight after a Friend or group of Friends have adopted a concern and taken action as well as before.

(c) Though management processes should not dominate, Quaker work which arises out of concern needs evaluation, development and support as much as any other enterprise, and this should surely include the search for guidance in a context of worship. Most of the

---

* "Thus John Woolman's 'concern' to visit England had been confirmed by the Monthly, then the Quarterly, and finally the Ministers and Elders of Philadelphia Yearly Meeting (decisions recorded in the 'certificate' which every minister carried with him as a sort of spiritual passport)" (J Ormerod Greenwood 1977, p30).

independent workers with whom we have discussed this either feel rather unsupported or look for it from fellow professionals rather than Quakers (and this has tended to be our personal practice). We believe there are ways in which Quaker bodies might support a concern which they do not intend to finance or manage. Some of these are suggested above. Others were discussed at the Friends World Committee for Consultation Conference on the Peace Testimony in January 2003. In some North American yearly meetings, a person seeking to test a possible concern will first ask for a clearness meeting of Friends with whom they can think it through. The meeting is held as a form of worship. If the concern is accepted, the person may also ask the committee to consider whether it is one which the whole meeting might share. That would lead to the creation of a support (or care) committee, giving emotional and spiritual support, prayer, and perhaps assistance with fundraising or practical needs; it may include members who are experienced in this specific area of concern. There may also be an oversight committee appointed, whose task is to receive reports and guide and admonish the concerned person if necessary. The meeting thus submits the concern to Quaker process, unites with it and demonstrates this in visible ways.

Another practice which has been revived from earlier times is the appointment of a spiritual or travelling companion (sometimes also referred to as the concerned Friend's "elder"). These Friends contribute to the work in logistical, emotional and spiritual ways, sometimes accompanying the Friend, or else keeping in close touch through modern means of communication (Margery Post Abbott & Peggy Senger Parsons 2004, section 4). Val Liveoak of Friends Peace Teams (USA) notes how very uneven Quaker meetings are in supporting the concerns of their members, and goes on to say, "It seems to me that these practices deserve close and regular consideration as ways to support and sustain peacemakers in the Friends' community" (Val Liveoak 2003, p8). It seems to us that they might also suggest ways in which Britain Yearly Meeting as a whole could own the informal Quaker work which it does not manage.

Chapter 4

Entertaining angels unawares

Leicester Quakers supporting asylum seekers, 2000–2005

by Rachel Carmichael

Be not forgetful to entertain strangers: for thereby some have entertained angels unawares.
Hebrews 13:2

For I was hungry, and ye gave me meat: I was thirsty, and ye gave me drink; I was a stranger, and ye took me in . . .

Background

Leicester is proud to be a multiracial city, which has over the years been enriched by people coming from many parts of the world. Currently more than a third of Leicester's residents are of black or minority ethnic origin. The many faith groups work well together, and there is a tradition of voluntary organisations co-operating with each other and with statutory agencies in responding to need. We have good structures, which help us work effectively.

Leicester is one of the places to which the National Asylum Support Service (NASS) has dispersed newly arrived asylum seekers since 2000, while they await a decision on their claim for asylum. From April 2000, a private agency had a contract with the Home Office to provide 430 beds for asylum seekers. Many were placed in a large hotel (now closed) and in consortium and private sector accommodation. Since May 2001 the Home Office has also had a contract with the City Council, Refugee Housing, and other private providers, to provide housing for asylum seeker families. Some opt to forgo NASS accommodation and live with friends or family.

In February 2005 it was estimated that there are approximately 1150 asylum seekers in Leicester, including those in NASS accommodation, those living with family or friends, and those supported by social services. No-one knows how many refugees there are here, because once asylum seekers receive refugee status, they are free to move where they want to. We do know that many destitute people who have been refused permission to stay by the system are trying to make a life here. And we know that because Leicester is such a pleasant place, they usually want to stay here, which is not always the case with other cities!

Quakers getting involved

Leicester Meeting has been involved with asylum seekers in a number of ways. In May 2000, when I was clerk of the meeting, I realised that the meeting might want to raise our voice about the injustices of the asylum system. The meeting agreed our support in principle for a welcoming approach, which meant we could take initiatives, and work with others. In the last five years many members of the meeting have responded in different ways.

We became involved with other organisations at that time, when as clerk I represented the meeting on the Leicester Asylum Seeker and Refugee Voluntary Sector Forum. At the first meeting I attended I heard of the concerns of asylum seekers that the food at the hotel was inappropriate (not surprisingly, in view of the seventeen different nationalities living there). I offered the meeting house kitchen for cooking, then realised that my own kitchen would be more convenient since I knew when it would be free, and in the next few weeks I welcomed Fatima and a number of her women friends to cook their own home food there, taking it back in ice cream cartons to feed their compatriots at the hotel. This led to friendships, and to a group of asylum seekers starting to come to meeting for worship. Many meals have since been cooked, using recipes from England and other countries. On Christmas Day two families enjoyed entertaining families and groups of asylum seekers. After one meal, for four asylum seekers from different countries, a discussion with a group of (non-Quaker) friends led to a friendship developing between two Iraqi doctors and four of the group.

Fatima and her family

Our early contacts were with Fatima and a number of other residents of the hotel. Fatima told us:

> *I had to come to England as a political asylum. It has been a pleasure meeting the Friends from the Friends Meeting House. It's no wonder it is called "Friends Meeting House". I cannot express my gratitude for what my friends, too many to mention, have done – the many ways they have tried to help me and my family feel at home. It's been financial support, moral support and spiritual support everywhere. I've even had a chance to polish up my English. So even if I were to go back home after this experience I won't really settle ever because I feel so much at home here, and I'd still wish to be near the family I have made here from the Quakers Friends Meeting House. It has not been easy not being able to help myself the way I usually do when I am at home. To an extent I've found it hard to accept the gifts I have been given by Friends, because I feel so useless with not being able to return the favours. Overall it has not been easy being here as an asylum seeker.*

Worship and social activities

In the early months, a number of asylum seekers came to meeting for worship with Fatima. Some of them joined our children's meeting groups to talk about their experiences. Feedback from the children suggests that it was a very powerful meeting for everyone. They are not coming often now, as they explore other ways of worship, but Fatima and her children came regularly and joined our many activities, until they moved to another city. Introductions have been made to museums and other free activities in Leicester. Sheila Mosley is a keen folk singer, and has taken a number of asylum seekers to folk clubs. From this it has become clear that one of the Iranian men is a wonderful singer and with her help he has given concerts in Leicester and Nottingham. Now Sheila is heavily involved with Farside Music, a grass roots opportunity for people from all over the world to play music together, which meets at the YMCA every Sunday evening.

Pretik, (India), Farhad, (Afghanistan), and Sheila (England) playing at 'Farside Music', Leicester.

She found funding from Radio Leicester, the City Council and individuals to buy musical instruments to loan to asylum seekers, and give them the chance to forget their traumas in the joy of sharing again the music from home. A recent Farside Music concert brought together Kurdish musicians and a group of Morris dancers, giving Kurdish people a chance to participate in English dance, and English people to share in Kurdish dancing.

The meeting has welcomed asylum seekers to our New Year party and garden parties, where croquet and circle dancing have proved hits. Visits to cinemas prove a wonderful lift to people who cannot afford to pay the entrance themselves.

Support and "accompanying"

This has taken many different forms, with different members of the meeting responding in different ways. A Friend who taught English as a second language for many years in Africa helped a group of asylum seekers with materials for a number of months, so that they could help their colleagues in the hotel.

Through Loughborough Meeting we were asked to find a young mother to visit an expectant mother from Palestine living in Loughborough but sent to Leicester as her baby was imminent. Two successful visits to their home were arranged.

Two 80-year-old Friends, Mark and Erika Monger, have provided counselling, friendship and practical support for three of Fatima's sisters. Ayesha told us:

When you're at home, in your comfort zone, it would never occur to you that one day you might end up being a stranger in a foreign land. When it happens to you, then you realise that you are no different to everyone else who has been a victim of political instability. You learn to humble yourself for at this point you have no control whatsoever of your life. You become scared and vulnerable. Being in contact with the Friends has made the burden we carry less. In the midst of all our disappointments we have been given a ray of hope through the love shown.

One Friday Fatima had a phone call from home to say that close friends had been murdered. She and her family were due to go to the Leicester Quaker Monthly Meeting camp in Derbyshire for the Bank Holiday. Fatima did not go, as in her country mourning and grief consume the whole person. The girls had a rich time at camp and only heard the terrible news on their return home.

■ *When things were getting particularly difficult for the family, we had a phone call at 6am one morning from the mother of the family speaking from her home, asking for help with sorting out some special problems. In recent months there has been no news from family members left behind.*

Money and food

Asylum seekers have to live on 70% of unemployment benefit, or, when in full board accommodation in 2000, on a £10 voucher each week. Often the vouchers were delayed, sent to the wrong address, or carried the wrong name. Maternity benefit is only paid weeks after the baby is born. Visits have to be made to lawyers and to immigration offices all over the country at a few days' notice. In theory, fares for essential visits are paid through the lawyer, but often not in time to purchase tickets. Phone calls home have to be paid for out of the £10 a week. Sometimes vouchers did not arrive, and people were left starving. Due to pressure from refugee groups and churches, the voucher system was abolished, but bureaucratic delays are still a nightmare. This is a bare outline of some of the elements of our traumatising and unjust system.

Leicester Meeting has made emergency collections to give to the Red Cross to buy food for asylum seekers who are starving. Two Friends, who had been refugees themselves sixty years ago, gave money from their pensions for phone cards for more than a year to our special family so that they could keep contact with home. The meeting decided one year that the annual collection after meeting for worship for Amnesty International should be allocated for urgent needs to asylum seekers. This raised £475, and was needed soon for a number of different emergencies. It was agreed that one asylum seeker, with three pre-school children, needed to get out of their one tiny hotel room, and join the playgroups that meet at the meeting house on four mornings a week. We agreed to pay for the family to join the playgroups by subsidising the fee for them on those days. Many generous individual donations have been and continue to be made to meet emergency situations, including a gift of a buggy for the new baby, and support for the whole family to go to the headquarters of the National Asylum Support Service at Croydon, in the hope that their asylum status could be resolved.

■ *Since 2001 we have had regular collections of toiletries, food and money to give to different organisations appealing for help for destitute asylum seekers.*

■ *Zainab says: "Being on the receiving end of your help constantly has never been easy for me. But one thing for certain is that I've learnt from your generosity immensely, and my daughter and I will be better people and citizens in that respect in our future life. Thank you."*

Clothing, furniture, and equipment

Initially arrivals in this country need warm clothing. This we have tried to provide. When asylum seekers get "permission to stay" or "extended leave to remain", they have to move out of the NASS assisted accommodation hotels or hostels within two weeks. Emails to members of the meeting proved a wonderful way of clarifying needs, and getting responses. When Fatima was moved into a flat, then into a council house, in order to leave her younger sisters in the flat, we were able to collect furniture and equipment which made a big contribution. Other friends of Friends were also very generous, though it is a delicate balance offering gifts to friends. Sometimes they may not really want the beautiful chair we value! A sewing machine was provided for the hotel, and we even provided a paper pattern, cut out of newspaper, for the women in the hotel to make pinafores from donated fabric.

The requirement to move out of NASS accommodation immediately still presents acute problems. Despite offers of guarantees of rental from Friends, letting agencies will still not let new refugees rent their properties, as the only references they can provide are from NASS, their previous "landlord". So at a time when the new refugees should be rejoicing in their status, they often become homeless.

Dealing with the system

■ *Asylum seekers are at the mercy of an inadequate, deliberately restrictive and bureaucratic system. They have to comply immediately with requests to go for interview, at pain of being deported if they do not go. Often when they arrive at the interview, there is some error in the bureaucracy's paperwork. You go to Mansfield, Castle Donington or Glasgow. The barrister looks at your papers and asks "Are you from South Africa?" "No, I'm from Somalia." Case adjourned. Asylum seekers who do not speak English are particularly disadvantaged. We have all helped in different ways by going to a hearing or visiting lawyers, and by writing letters of support. Transport has been provided at a moment's notice for visits to family members just arrived at Oakington Reception Centre, or to Feltham Immigration Centre.*

■ *Zainab's experience speaks for many of them: "I entered the UK as an asylum seeker seeking refuge from the situation at home. Ironically I was taken to Oakington Detention Centre where I spent eight days and shared a room with about ten depressed, lonely, hopeless, frightened and even suicidal asylum seekers. This only added to my list of horrific experiences from back home."*

We have supported by letter and phone an Iranian asylum seeker who was imprisoned in Exeter, who has also been supported by his local meeting. He has taken much comfort from knowing that friends in our meeting are thinking of him. Besides these "reconciling" activities, we also have a "prophetic" task. A lawyer member of our meeting, now living in Birmingham, has taken on special cases for us, as there are now only two legal practices in Leicester prepared to work on immigration cases since the government has put so many restrictions on the way they are allowed to operate. Leicester Meeting and individual members have written letters to the Home Office ministers about some of the many injustices in the system, citing examples we are concerned about. We have also written individual letters to our MPs, supporting the Oxfam campaign to end the voucher system.

Links with other organisations

We have joined with others to "identify those who can make change" We have two representatives on the Faiths Support Group for Asylum Seekers and Refugees, which developed the Welcome Day Centre Project, based at Leicester Cathedral, at which two of our members serve as volunteers fortnightly. We joined in monthly visits to the International Hotel, organised by the Faiths Support Group, until it closed in October 2004.

I represent Leicester Meeting on the Voluntary Sector Forum on Asylum Seekers and Refugees, which I now chair. In this capacity I have written letters on behalf of the Forum to the Lord Chancellor, local MPs, the Secretary of State, and many others from 2002 to 2004, protesting about planned legislation and legal aid restrictions. Unfortunately these were usually voices crying in the wilderness.

The Voluntary Sector Forum has merged with the Leicester Multi Agency Forum for Asylum Seekers and Refugees to consider issues of concern and development, and I co-chair this group. Through these fora we keep in touch with the current situation, and work with other like-minded people.

Pilot project

I used to work with the Leicester Volunteer Centre, and Voluntary Action Leicester (VAL), of which it is part, and with them developed a grant application for a befriending scheme for asylum seekers. We attracted funding from three charitable trusts, including one Quaker Trust. This project, Amity, used the Leicester Quaker Meeting experience as a pilot scheme for what can be done if individuals or a group get involved with asylum seekers. A full time paid worker was employed by VAL for three years to recruit and train volunteers to link up with new arrivals in Leicester. We found that appropriate matching was not as easy as it had been in the natural flowing community of a Quaker meeting, as young women were the main volunteer group, and single young men the main asylum seekers group. But the advice and support of the worker was invaluable, as were the unforeseen developments – three lively Refugee Weeks, and a volunteer group who produced a number of issues of a special magazine, *Alive*.

Destitution

In mid summer 2003 Refugee Action called a special meeting of the Multi Agency Forum to tell us about their great concern that a number of their clients who were in emergency accommodation were having their cases reviewed under Section 55; by 14 July they had received several negative support decisions. This meant that Refugee Action had to send letters to these clients telling them they were to be evicted within seven days, with no housing, no continuing support, and no permission to work.

The gathering started to explore possible solutions, including setting up an emergency accommodation centre, accommodating people in private homes, and linking with groups who might help. Further discussion made it clear that despite guidelines for providing accommodation in private homes being drawn up, no organisation was able to take responsibility for such a scheme, with the potential risks to both asylum seekers and hosts. Meanwhile St Margaret's Parochial Church Council considered whether a Day Centre could be based in their church hall, and kindly agreed that this would be possible twice a week. The group agreed in principle to welcome and accept an offer from Toc H (a Christian organisation working with communities to promote friendship and service, confront prejudice and practise reconciliation) to work with us on the project. An Advisory Group was set up to work with Toc H, and Toc H set in

Leicester Multi Agency Forum for Asylum Seekers and Refugees, with Rachel Carmichael co-chairing (third from right).

motion the recruitment of the project worker. This would use up the tentative staffing budget, so it was vital to start finding other resources urgently. The Day Centre opened in December, on Mondays and Fridays, offering support and advice, and signposting to other agencies in Leicester. We offered hot food, and dried food and tins to take away. An office base was rented at the Cathedral Centre from April 2004.

During the next few months more than £6000 was given by over thirty churches, synagogues, and a number of individuals. Our meeting had a special collection, which raised £450, and Oakham Meeting sent £100. Refugee Action donated £5000 for start up costs. These donations were vital to keeping the centre operational. Volunteers to help in the centre were recruited and trained on a joint course with Refugee Action.

Increasing demands

By March 2004, 46 of Refugee Action's clients had had to leave their emergency accommodation, and the Day Centre had had 21 clients who had called, from four to eight on any one day. It is very painful to close the door on someone whom you know has nowhere to sleep, but the Advisory Group had sadly to decide 'under no circumstances are we to become involved in any housing offer on a voluntary basis'. By mid October 134 clients had visited the centre, from nineteen different countries – Afghanistan, Albania, Algeria, Congo, England, India, Iran, Jamaica, Mongolia, Nepal, Pakistan, Poland, Serbia, Slovakia, Somalia, Sri Lanka, Turkey, Yemen, Zimbabwe. Among many things they needed were food, advocacy, physical support, explanation of letters, advice on filling in forms, help with accommodation, and medical advice.

We are increasingly worried about the number of destitute asylum seekers in our city, and the Voluntary Sector Forum carried out a survey for four weeks in January and February 2005 to try to identify how many there are. All the agencies visited by destitute asylum seekers participated. The results show that about 170 asylum seekers are destitute in Leicester, some newly made destitute, some for longer periods up to four years. The majority are living with friends, but a few are sleeping in car parks, corridors, doorways, streets, parks and the train station.

We are not yet sure how organisations will respond together to this information, but are grateful to have been involved in a co-operative and practical way in showing that we care for those in our city who are left destitute through no fault of their own, and after many terrible experiences.

How Leicester Friends have worked

Some of the issues we are concerned about we have taken to Preparative Meeting (the local Quaker business meeting). When we have needed to identify those who can make change, such as politicians, we have tried to help them understand our concerns. Otherwise there has been no formal organisation at work. Each individual has done what seems within their powers, and what seems right to them. But some good principles have been at work. We have kept each other carefully informed about the needs, and what we are doing. We have shared our concerns about what is happening to individual asylum seekers, and given each other, as well as them, support. Those of us appointed by Preparative Meeting to distribute the "Amnesty Fund" have discussed and agreed the priorities. We have responded pragmatically as has seemed right, joining in this concern as an act of shared faith and an opportunity to live out our testimonies.

Our commitment has lasted more than five years already, and will not end. We have kept in constant touch with our friends. We have helped a teenager develop her CV as she approaches school leaving. An Iranian refugee who has been in touch with the meeting for five years, and who is now doing a PhD at Leicester University, asked for help from our consultant eye surgeon member for advice about the worrying loss of sight of a friend in Iran. Two teenage Friends collected chocolates and biscuits at school for Christmas treats for visitors to the Welcome Project. Recently two Friends heard that a computer was needed by one of our friends for her law A Level studies, and gave her one they did not need. We have enjoyed shared theatre visits, and outings to the zoo. A student member of our meeting is writing her dissertation on the view of asylum seekers portrayed by the tabloid press.

We have joined in Kurdish and Persian New Year's Day celebrations. We have written letters guaranteeing hospitality, and rejoice this Easter when Turkish refugees can therefore give a holiday to their family whom they have not seen for years. We have received job satisfaction from helping with an international problem about which we often feel so powerless. We have shared our blessedly safe homes and material goods. We have learned to be very grateful for our democracy, however imperfect.

We have learnt what it is like to be a refugee in a strange country. We have learnt how powerless asylum seekers are within the system, and how purposeless life can be without work. We have learned about the countries from which the asylum seekers come. We have shared a ministry of presence, by standing beside those in trouble. We have tried to live out our testimonies to equality and truth.

And we have gained many rich friendships. Ayesha told us:

When I came to Leicester, I was remitted to my two sisters and days later I met the Quaker Friends. They brought into my life what I hadn't known in a long time – a social life. Words cannot express how much I appreciate everything they do for me and my family. As asylum seekers we have an endless list of social, spiritual and financial needs and it is great to know that we're not alone in our trials. I've realised that 'A friend in need is a friend indeed'. God Bless.

■ *I developed this chapter along with friends made among asylum seekers and refugees. At the final drafting stage some of them became so fearful of retribution being taken against relatives back home that all personal stories have had to be adapted, and names changed. The text in italics is original. I sympathise deeply with this fear of the long arm of tyranny, and am sorry that it has made this picture less vivid.*

Chapter 5

Responding to Conflict in the North Caucasus

by Chris Hunter

In February 1995 I was present at a most extraordinary congress on the outskirts of Moscow – the annual meeting of the Committee of Soldiers' Mothers of Russia. The congress took place two months after the first Russian troops were sent into Grozny and the bombs began to fall on the city and its inhabitants. The Russian mothers at the congress were appalled at what their politicians and military leaders were doing in Chechnya in the name of "restoring constitutional order" and horrified that their sons were being used to do it. They were also painfully aware of the lack of preparation, equipment and even adequate clothing provided to these 18 and 19-year-old conscripts, whose corpses were already being sent home in the hundreds. "If our generals are so concerned about constitutional order in Chechnya, then why don't they send their own sons there to restore it?" asked one angry and anxious mother. Others stated that they were not prepared to stay at home and wait for the news of their sons' deaths for a dirty war they did not believe in – they would have to go to Chechnya themselves to bring their boys home. Chechen mothers had also been invited to speak at the congress. They spoke of the terrible destruction and suffering of the civilian population in Chechnya, of how the capital city was being carpet bombed, and of the thousands of inhabitants – Chechens, Russians and other nationalities – trapped in basements without food or water.

Many people from Chechen women's, youth and human rights groups had shared with me their stories and accounts of the devastating effect of the war in Chechnya over the previous weeks. I was working as a Quaker Peace & Service (QPS) representative in Moscow, and so was viewed as a representative of the international community. Many of these people felt that the population in Chechnya was completely isolated and forgotten, and they saw it as their task to alert international opinion to the horror unfolding in the republic. They believed that if the truth of what was happening to ordinary, peace-loving inhabitants in Chechnya was known, then people everywhere would react and unite to put a stop to such a senseless war.

I felt deeply moved and saddened by the stories and reports that I heard. In my role as a Quaker representative it felt important first to listen to these traumatic and tragic stories, which the tellers needed so much to convey to receptive ears and hearts. I felt very much a sense of spiritual responsibility, as Brian Phillips describes in the first chapter. Why should people in Chechnya be left alone to experience such devastation? What could I, and others, do to help and to support their efforts to find solutions?

For two months I had participated in prayer vigils, public meetings, round tables and conferences in Moscow, calling for an immediate cessation of violence and the restoration of peace. Prominent Russian politicians and civil society leaders also took part. But such activities were having little impact. On the other hand, the Russian soldiers' mothers and Chechen women whom I met in Moscow showed such spirit and compassion for the young

Russian soldiers' mothers march

conscripts and civilians suffering in Chechnya that I wondered how these dynamic and courageous voices for peace could be better heard. A small group of us met together during a break at the soldiers' mothers' congress and came up with an idea for a Mothers' March for Life and Compassion from Moscow to Grozny. Our small basement QPS office in Moscow became the coordination centre for the march (a kind of press office, planning and logistics centre, national and international liaison and fundraising base all rolled into one) and on 8 March, International Women's Day, 1995 the marchers set off from Red Square. Soldiers' mothers, Chechen women, Buddhist monks, local Russian Quakers, representatives from Jewish and Russian Orthodox faiths walked through central Moscow, beating drums and chanting, and followed by dozens of journalists and several TV camera crews. As the distance to Grozny was well over 1000 miles, large stretches of the march were covered in buses. The buses stopped at Russian cities and towns along the way to inform people why we were marching, through local media, vigils and public meetings.

About two weeks later around 200 marchers crossed over the border from Ingushetia into Chechnya. Bombs were pounding the small settlement of Bamut a few miles to the south. As we entered the first Chechen village of Sernovodsk, hundreds of inhabitants lined the streets to meet and cheer the marchers, handing us warm bread and salt as a traditional welcome. After weeks and months of isolation and terror, here were people from afar risking their lives to show they cared about what was happening in Chechnya. Following speeches at a public meeting local people put us up in their homes for the night, before we set off deeper into war-torn Chechnya the following morning. A similar welcome awaited us in Samashki, but that day we needed to press on to the regional centre of Achkhoi Martan. A military roadblock prevented us from doing so. Russian soldiers were instructed to form two rings around the marchers and we were held there until late into the night.

Animated discussions with Russian military personnel ensued, interspersed with humour and smiles on weary faces of marchers, soldiers and officers. Away from their seniors, some Russian servicemen expressed their support for the march and hoped they could soon go home from this war that they wanted to have no part in. Russian soldiers' mothers sought information to lead them to their sons' units so they could challenge the commander and bring their boys home. Chechen women described to the soldiers the devastation that the war had brought to their lives and saw at close hand the terrible conditions that the soldiers themselves were living under.

In the middle of the night the few foreign male marchers were lifted out of the crowd by special forces under glaring lights and taken to a dark corner behind a row of tanks. Russian and Chechen women tried to hold on to us and pleaded for us to be released, afraid for what might happen to us. We were searched, there was more talking and then everyone was herded into buses and driven back to Ingushetia.

Personal security was an important factor and concern for me during the march and during the following years of working in Chechnya, as it was for many others. The personal risk of such work and witness was often great. The conviction I felt that I should be there with people from Chechnya and Russia at such desperate times and initiating activities that offered hope and relief, reconciled me to this personal risk. Although I inevitably felt fear at times, mainly before the trips into Chechnya rather than during them, the prompting and openings of the Spirit to do this work were clear, particularly at the most crucial times, and they sustained me. Fortunately colleagues, family and friends understood and shared the conviction that led me to being there, though it sometimes, understandably, caused them anxiety too. During the march, an update of our situation was passed on through friends of the monks to my Quaker Peace & Service colleague in Moscow, Patricia Cockrell. The message that some of the marchers had been beaten up was relayed bluntly over a crackling line in Russian as "ikh izbili: they've been beaten up" and heard as "ikh ubili: they've been killed". Patricia had gastritis at the time, and this condition together with the news, which seemingly referred to all the marchers, caused her body to go into a state of shock, with trembling and sharp stomach pains. Fortunately we were soon able to confirm that everyone was still alive, although a group of Buddhist monks who had been on the march had indeed been held and beaten by Russian troops in another part of Chechnya.

Most of the marchers returned to Sernovodsk from Ingushetia to plan further efforts to bring the war and its tragic consequences to the attention of the public in Russia and abroad. The TV camera crews and many of the journalists were still with us, and so news of our activities and the soldiers' mothers' efforts to free their sons was being broadcast throughout Russia and several European countries. While we waited to continue the march to Grozny, I was able to network with groups and individuals who were deeply motivated to make a positive change to what was happening around them. I was able to provide some with video and photo cameras to record the atrocities being committed without the knowledge of people outside Chechnya. I collated information that Chechen women travelled bravely around Chechnya to collect, and sent it to relevant bodies such as Amnesty International, who used it to publish urgent appeals and updates, and to relevant United Nations departments and international peace movement representatives.

The town of Samashki, which the march had passed through days earlier, was surrounded by Russian forces as we waited in Sernovodsk and a brutal massacre of civilians took place there. Shortly afterwards Chechen women accompanied me and a Russian Quaker and his colleague to the town, to speak with survivors and hear personal accounts of the horrors that happened there. We met many more people from the town who arrived to seek refuge in Sernovodsk, some of whom had been tortured. The scale of the mindless violence and cruelty that was crippling the bodies and lives of many of the people I was meeting brought home to me in a very real and tangible way the tremendous potential for barbarity of human beings. I felt very close then to what George Fox had described as "an ocean of Darkness and Death" and for a time experienced a terrible loss of faith in a human race that was capable of such acts. I was reassured by the spirit and generosity of the people around me in Sernovodsk, who helped to restore my faith in humanity, and to see again the work of Fox's "ocean of Light and Love" that was keeping hope and even humour alive in such a desperate environment. Continuing to seek and respond to the openings of the Spirit seemed the only way for me to make sense of what was happening.

In the summer of 1995, I worked with Rachel Brett and colleagues at QUNO (Quaker United Nations Office) in Geneva and with the International Peace Bureau to bring two Chechen women and

two Russian soldiers' mothers to Geneva. We spoke to members of
the United Nations Human Rights Committee, meeting to discuss
human rights in the Russian Federation at the time, and with other
UN, governmental and nongovernmental bodies. Our presence
and testimonies meant that the official Russian government policy
to paper over human rights abuses in Chechnya was undermined,
and the truth of Samashki and other atrocities was brought out into
the open. With the help of peace groups around Europe and QCEA
(Quaker Council for European Affairs) in Brussels, I was able to
organise further speaking tours for Russian and Chechen women who
were courageously working for peace in their communities. We spoke
to the European Parliament and national parliamentary committees,
politicians and dignitaries such as Mme Danielle Mitterand, and to
the press and to peace and human rights groups. Back in Russia, those
of us who had coordinated the march brought together a group of
Russian, Chechen and international peace and human rights activists
and scholars to publish accounts of our work for peace in Chechnya
and Russia in the form of a book called *Chechnya in My Heart* (Karta
journal, 1997).

Persistently raising awareness about a concern and using
instruments of international law to promote justice and positive
change can be very effective, as Chapter 6 of this book demonstrates.
The challenge of using such instruments to overcome the injustice of
violent conflict in a particular region or country can be particularly
complex, especially when an influential nation is involved as one of
the main perpetrators of violence and oppression. Leaders of powerful
nations are reluctant to risk upsetting their political, economic and
security relations with an important strategic partner for the sake of
defending human rights. And so as the conflict in Chechnya enters
its eleventh year, the Chechens and others caught up in the war
remain in many ways victims of the macro-political, global situation.
Western leaders are unwilling or unable to effect serious change on
Russia's policy in Chechnya. It has been made more difficult still
following the war in Iraq. Russian leaders deflect any criticism of their
methods in Chechnya by maintaining that they are fighting global
terror, just as the USA and Britain are doing in Iraq. As is so often the
case in other parts of the world, the violent "solutions" imposed on

people in Chechnya are doing nothing to foster stability or to reduce violence. We are witnessing the very opposite, as extremists inflict instability and suffering increasingly beyond Chechnya's borders in neighbouring Russian regions and in the capital Moscow. The theatre siege in Moscow in 2002 and the Beslan school tragedy in 2004 are two prominent and tragic examples. The work that my colleagues and I developed in Chechnya has focused increasingly on supporting local initiatives for peace: offering training and support for peacebuilding initiatives and assisting and empowering people of all ages to deal with and survive the trauma and suffering of war.

At the same time as helping to raise awareness of how war was affecting people's lives in Chechnya, I worked with people on the ground there to arrange practical support to those who had lost their homes, possessions and loved ones. The brothers of one family I met in Sernovodsk had been driving into Grozny, dodging the bullets in a 15-year-old Lada Estate to bring fresh bread and supplies to some of the thousands of people still trapped in basements as the fighting and bombing thundered above them. I met many such individuals, whose courage and drive to help was inspiring, but who had access to few resources and so were limited in what they could do. I appealed to international humanitarian agencies, which generally considered Chechnya to be too dangerous a place to work. I offered to use the networks I had been building to distribute their food, clothing and other assistance without the need for them to risk being present there themselves. Oxfam, World Vision International, American Friends Service Committee, Quaker Peace & Service and other organisations obliged.

As such work gained momentum, financial constraints in Britain Yearly Meeting and cuts in centrally funded work meant that QPS would soon no longer be able to employ representatives in Russia. Patricia Cockrell and I had written an application to a funding body of the European Commission, "Technical Assistance to CIS countries" (TACIS), which would enable us to continue our activities, including the work in the North Caucasus, peace education and our support for conscientious objectors in Russia. We needed an international partner to apply for the grant, and for several reasons QPS was unable to play that role. The German sister organisation of QPS, Quäker Hilfe, subsequently agreed to be our international partner and to support our work in this way. Shortly before the deadline for submitting the TACIS grant however, the clerk of the QPS committee in London to which we were responsible contacted us to say that a minute made by the committee meant that we were not allowed to apply for the European Commission grant. Patricia and I met in her central Moscow flat, the grant application spread out covering half of the floor, and deliberated on what was to be done. The deadline for the application was that same day. The committee must have had its reasons for forbidding us to submit the proposal, we considered, but at the same time we were aware daily of the great needs that the grant would allow us the resources to answer to.

Neither of us had previous experience of disobeying our employers in this way, but conscience and leadings of the Spirit urged overwhelmingly that we do it. This was after weeks of discussion, discerning and quiet contemplation: we decided to submit the application and hurried to the European Commission offices, hastily made the required number of copies and handed them in just in time. We were called by QPS to a meeting in London shortly afterwards, where we all spoke honestly and openly about the situation. Having listened intently to everyone, QPS general secretary Andrew Clark referred to the committee minute and to the elders of Balby, who had affirmed the predominance of the Spirit over the letter. The decision was made to continue supporting us as QPS representatives and to accept the decision we had made. The TACIS grant application was approved by the Commission, and on receiving it, we set up a new organisation called the Centre for Peacemaking and Community Development (CPCD). QPS continued supporting us as representatives until the new international Quaker body Friends House Moscow was opened in 1996. QPS continued supporting me as a Friend working under concern for around two further years. Since that arrangement ceased, my monthly meeting in Leeds has provided support to me as a Friend under concern.

CPCD became the structure for implementing the activities of the one-year TACIS grant, and it also provided the framework for new projects in the North Caucasus. In 1996, I helped to facilitate an international youth conference "Peace in Caucasia" in Yalta, which brought together young people working for peace and justice from all over the region and other parts of Russia. We developed plans there for a peacebuilding network in the North Caucasus to provide ongoing training in peacebuilding skills and coordination of peace and humanitarian projects. During the months I spent in Chechnya I had become aware of the detrimental effects that the war was having on the psychological health of people there as it entered its second year. We discussed this at the conference in Yalta, and a group of us resolved to explore ways in which we could provide assistance to those most in need of psychosocial support.

During the months ahead, my Chechen colleague Adlan and I worked with local partners and authorities in Chechnya to register the organisation and plan the new projects and activities. At the same time, I wrote funding proposals and applied to donors in Europe. In January 1997 we held an international youth conference in the ruined Chechen capital Grozny to further raise awareness of the situation and develop practical responses to assist the local population and support the excellent ideas and initiatives of local activists. We supported a group of the conference participants to set up a Chechen youth group, Laman Az (Voice of the Mountains), which continues its relief and education work in Grozny today with support from UN agencies. Many of the conference participants remained behind afterwards to help monitor Chechnya's elections, which saw Aslan Maskhadov elected as President with international and Russian recognition. Russian troops had been withdrawn from the republic since a peace agreement between Russian and Chechen leaders several months earlier. Another presidential candidate, Shamil Basayev, who had orchestrated the siege of a hospital in southern Russia as a call to Russian politicians for peace talks, visited the conference, responding to our open invitation to all of the candidates. We conducted a dialogue with him in plenary about our aims and efforts to help build peace in Chechnya by peaceful means, and listened to his views on the situation and relations with Russia. Participants from Russia afterwards, used to media reports that demonised Basayev, had private discussions with him which were respectful and ended with a good degree of common understanding.

In the spring of 1997 the Chechen Ministry of Health agreed to loan the building of a former children's sanatorium to CPCD in return

Little Star performers

for our repairing damage inflicted to it during the war, installing a new heating system and redecorating the buildings. The building, right on the edge of Grozny in a tranquil setting surrounded by trees and fields, became the children's psychological rehabilitation centre, Little Star. We invited international experts to train local teachers and nurses in psychosocial assistance. They became our new staff members and worked in Grozny schools with children, teachers and parents, identifying children with particularly high levels of psychological stress. We brought these children to the Little Star Centre by bus every day after school (before lunch as the schools worked in a shift system) for several hours of activities. We aimed to create a safe, creative and supporting environment for the children at the new centre, to allow the children to gently unwind, open up to each other and the counsellors, and in many cases to remember what it was to play and to have fun. Activities included art, dancing, simulation games, theatre and festivals, as well as individual consultations with the counsellors. Camilla Carr and Jon James, friends of mine who had done similar work with children in the UK, came out to live with us in Grozny and to work at the Little Star Centre. Through regular consultation with the parents, we observed that many of the symptoms of stress and psychological trauma among the children such as sleeplessness, recurring nightmares, hyperactivity or antisocial behaviour, were abating.

In early July 1997, when the work of Little Star and our other peacebuilding and humanitarian programmes was gradually growing and developing, all of us at CPCD and many others in Chechnya and around the world were shocked at the news of Jon and Camilla's kidnapping. Armed gunmen burst into the house where our team was living in Grozny in the middle of the night and took Jon and Camilla away in blindfolds. I had just arrived in Cornwall for a break and so, not for the last time, narrowly escaped being abducted too. It was difficult to take in the news at first, but I immediately made journey plans back to Moscow and Grozny. I met with British Embassy staff in Moscow and with Chechen President Aslan Maskhadov, law enforcing agencies, colleagues and anyone else who might be able to help back in Chechnya. Such efforts, which included public appeals for help through television and other media, were complemented by the campaign of Jon and Camilla's families in the UK and efforts by the British government in Moscow. Finally, following fourteen months of captivity, at times in appalling conditions, Camilla and Jon were released. When I met Camilla at Brize Norton RAF base after their release, her first question was "How are the children at Little Star?" Jon and Camilla used mutual support, tai chi, chi kung and yoga techniques to survive their ordeal. They have both met with colleagues from Chechnya since, and Camilla leads sessions on art, movement and other creative skills at our regular retreat seminars for the sixty psychologists and counsellors working at Little Star today. Camilla was raped by one of her captors, but ever since her release she has affirmed that she feels no hatred towards any of the men who held her and Jon captive. She has talked about the desperation and trauma that their captors too had suffered in the war, and is able to forgive them for what they did to her. Camilla and Jon have inspired thousands of people through talks and interviews since their release, and through their participation in The Forgiveness Project, which informs the public of their and other examples of people managing to forgive what some may consider to be unforgivable.

Jon, Camilla and I all understood the risk of living and working in Chechnya. Their kidnapping and another in Ingushetia at the same time marked the beginning of a period of numerous kidnappings by criminal groups, usually for ransom as in Jon and Camilla's case. Hundreds of Chechens were kidnapped too, but it was the several dozen abductions of foreigners that made the headlines around the world. Shortly after Jon and Camilla's release, four telecommunications workers, three of whom were from the UK, were found beheaded in Chechnya, several weeks after being abducted.

As the security situation deteriorated, many international organisations closed down their missions in the North Caucasus. The strength of CPCD was that the majority of workers and volunteers were local people who continued the work when international staff could no longer visit. This enhanced the trust of the local population who appreciated the evidence of commitment to a long-term approach. The strong partnership built up between international and local staff and volunteers at CPCD, and with our partners also plays a key role in our work.

The kidnappings and other crimes, fuelled by the devastating effects of the war, mass unemployment and economic disaster, marked the fall of Chechen society into a spiral of lawlessness that the new government was unable to control. The Russian authorities offered the Chechen government little support, and indeed impeded their attempts to help the republic back onto its feet. Extremist groups in Chechnya were becoming increasingly influential, and in 1999 such a group led an incursion into a region of neighbouring Dagestan. This triggered Moscow's decision, in September 1999, to send the troops back into Chechnya, this time "to combat terrorism". All CPCD staff members had to flee Chechnya for their safety, as did the rest of the population who had the means to do so. One of the Little Star counsellors met with our Ingushetia coordinator Murad, and so established contact through him with Adlan and me. We gradually found all the other counsellors, who also had fled to Ingushetia, and so we set about establishing small Little Star centres there to provide psychosocial support to children living in the tent camps for internally displaced people. These small centres or points were in tents, but nevertheless could provide the children with a creative, supportive space in their new lives in the refugee camps. As the military campaign gradually subsided in Chechnya, we were able to open further such points all over the republic, occupying classrooms in schools and a community building that we renovated in 2003. Our sixty psychologists and counsellors now all work in such centres in pairs, and in 2005 we will open a new purpose-built larger centre in Grozny to bring the children to for trips and for more intensive work to assist children with higher levels of trauma.

As the work of Little Star evolved over time, with vital financial support from our various donors and partners, so did many of our other projects, which are described briefly below. Today CPCD is a registered charitable company in the UK with a representation office in Moscow, branch offices in Chechnya and Ingushetia and smaller offices throughout the rest of the North Caucasus. We employ over 250 people, mainly locals, with our headquarters based in Bude, Cornwall. I have been living in the UK since 2001, since being unable to obtain a Russian visa due to my years of working in Chechnya and a new, suspicious Russian administration in Moscow. Although frustrating in some ways, having an unquestionable reason not to be able to continue living in Russia may well have saved me from burnout, which happens to many people living and working under constant stress in such an environment over long periods of time. Seven consecutive years in the field is sufficient in many ways, and continuing to manage the work and fundraise for it, to develop the structural framework for it from our UK base and to share my experience with people here and in other parts of Europe has also proved effective.

CPCD's work today focuses on developing local capacities for peace through programmes in peacebuilding, education, psychosocial support, humanitarian aid and reconstruction. Many of the peacebuilding activities in the North Caucasus centre around our Peacebuilding Network. This work includes conflict resolution, tolerance and human rights training for trainers, and seminars for young peacebuilders from the six North Caucasian republics, South Ossetia and North West Russia. Several dozen such trainers have now received training over several years and are themselves conducting seminars and other projects in their own republics. Projects developed between the republics include summer camps, youth exchanges incorporating conflict resolution training, round tables on peacebuilding themes, and conflict resolution in schools and universities. A project called "Russian North – North Caucasus" arranges youth camps for Russians and North Caucasians to help overcome prejudice. Other projects include youth cultural festivals and conflict resolution training with authorities such as traffic police. The network also provides support and training to local nongovernmental organisations (NGOs), facilitating relations between NGOs and journalists and promoting the reporting of conflict and peacebuilding activities in the media.

Dialogue work between civil society leaders from Russia and Chechnya has resulted in the participants creating a "Yalta Initiative for Peace in Chechnya" (YIPIC) dialogue coalition to explore ways to build understanding and move towards reconciliation. Joint peacebuilding projects are conducted, such as a Peace Prize Ceremony and an exhibition of Russian and Chechen children's drawings in Moscow in 2004. The Peace Prize was presented to distinguished Chechen and Russian peacebuilders at the Tretyakov Gallery and raised awareness of their work through the media. The children's drawing exhibition will be touring Europe in 2005. We have also conducted dialogue work with Ingush and Ossetian communities in the Prigorodny Region since 1995. We are beginning a new project there to bring children, young people and adults from both communities together through vocational skills training, creative workshops and training seminars.

Other CPCD programmes in Chechnya and Ingushetia provide practical support to internally displaced people and other vulnerable groups. This includes distributing food and hot meals, rebuilding damaged schools and medical buildings and running a grain mill and bakery. Our women's support centre in Ingushetia offers psychosocial, medical and general moral support to women. A further women's support centre and a men's support centre are planned in Grozny in 2005. A conflict resolution centre in Nazran, Ingushetia opened at the end of 2003 and provides training in conflict resolution, tolerance and human rights. Alternatives to Violence Project (AVP) workshops are held in Chechnya, Ingushetia and North Ossetia. CPCD supports the Chechen children's dance ensemble Daimohk, organising yearly European tours for the group.

In 2004, CPCD began peace education training for secondary school teachers in the Moscow Region. Over the year, around 140 teachers of the humanities participated in a series of seminars introducing principles and values for civic education. At these seminars, Russian trainers explained concepts of human rights, tolerance, democracy and conflict resolution, and methods of teaching these concepts to children. We estimate that around 8000 young people, aged 15 to 18, will benefit from this teaching. A conscientious objection consultant based at our Moscow office offers consultations for young men, providing them and their families with information and guidance on their rights as conscientious objectors.

My motivation for developing this work in Chechnya and Russia together with colleagues was and is a response to the great needs that I witnessed and an absence of adequate support from other sources. There is always a potential for despair, to think that after years of hard work the situation in Chechnya has barely improved, and in some ways has worsened since 1995. The lack of will on the governmental level in Russia to solve the many problems of the North Caucasus through peaceful means is a major reason for this and encourages the marginalisation of resistance groups, some of which are becoming ever more extreme in their responses.

What we are able to do is focus on peaceful solutions and to share and develop these with individuals and communities affected by violence. Decision and policy makers of the societies engaged in the armed conflict are often involved in this process. It is hard to quantify results of such work, but there is always a powerful potential for enacting positive change towards peace and justice with the many gifted and committed people who live in such difficult situations and who are still capable of envisioning a more positive and life-enhancing way of living.

All of us in our different ways are struggling to incorporate the tension of "living in the old city while building the new" (Britain Yearly Meeting Epistle, Exeter 1986). The situation in Chechnya in many ways mirrors and magnifies what is going on in each of us in our journey out of fear and ego towards love and "that of God within", to use the traditional Quaker expression. Wherever we are, we are called to do what we can to quicken the pace of this change for ourselves and for those we are privileged to come into contact with. As a Friend, I can think of nothing that brings more joy to the soul than helping to nurture the Light in such an environment as Chechnya beset by darkness and despair, through lending support to courageous initiatives of hope and healing.

■ *The "Centre for Peacemaking and Community Development", the CPCD company, ceased its activities at the end of December 2005, due to difficulties in the UK. The charity, using the similar name of "Centre for Peacebuilding and Community Development"' which was created to gradually take over the company's work, consequently did so sooner than planned, in January 2006. We therefore continue the work of CPCD in the North Caucasus, supported by a new UK structure. The many experienced and deeply committed local staff and partners in the region continue to run activities and programmes such as I have described.*

Chapter 6
Child Soldiers:
Implementing a Prophetic Vision through International Law

by Rachel Brett

Passions have at times run high among Friends in Britain contrasting the differences between "Central" or "Corporate" Quaker work, and individual Quaker concerns – usually disparaging the former. But what happens when the individual concern becomes corporate and needs the established structures to take it forward? The work of the Quaker UN Office, Geneva (QUNO) on child soldiers is an example of this: a tested individual Quaker concern being adopted as a corporate one and integrated into the "central" work.

Background

In 1978 a young French journalist, Nicolas Hulot, teamed up with a small French photography agency and produced a book about suffering children (Nicholas Hulot & Sipa-Press 1978). In it, they showed children dying from malnutrition, disease and injury caused by wars and natural disasters such as earthquakes and hurricanes. But they also showed children bearing arms – fighting and being trained to fight – in Ethiopia, Cambodia, Lebanon, Vietnam, Angola, Mozambique, Western Sahara and Kurdistan, Palestinian children being trained in the refugee camps in Lebanon, and also the militarisation of children in Northern Ireland. This book was shown to Dorothea Woods, a member of Geneva Monthly Meeting in Switzerland, by some friends of hers. Shortly afterwards she discovered another book, Peter Townsend's *The Smallest Pawns in the Game* (1980), which, in her own words, strengthened Hulot's "cry of conscience". *

---

* Dorothea E Woods: "Children bearing and using military arms", January 1980 (unpublished paper). It seems that Dorothea saw Peter Townsend's book prior to its publication.

In January 1979, Dorothea wrote to the Clerk of Geneva Monthly Meeting asking that the question of children bearing military arms be put on the agenda of Monthly Meeting. Writing a year later, she herself described what happened:

> When considering what concern might best be linked with the International Year of the Child [1979], the Geneva Monthly Meeting thought that the historic peace testimony of Quakers gave them a responsibility to try to do something about the children bearing arms in civil wars, in wars for independence, and even in the international wars of our time. . . . Our concern for these children came before the quarterly meeting of French-speaking Switzerland and then before Switzerland Yearly Meeting.

Switzerland Yearly Meeting (in June 1979) minuted:

> In this International Year of the Child, we wish to go on record against the practice of training children to kill and maim other human beings. We regret that the United Nations Declaration on the Rights of the Child offers no protection even against the use of children in open fighting. We encourage the United Nations and the international organisations to press for measures against the participation of children in military training and action.

Edna Legg, the clerk of Geneva Monthly Meeting, spoke to this concern at the Triennial Meeting of the Friends World Committee for Consultation (FWCC) in August 1979. The Triennial minuted:

> Edna P Legg has brought before us the concern of the Switzerland Yearly Meeting that Friends should register their abhorrence of the widespread involvement of children in military training and even in active combat. We unite with this concern and ask yearly meetings to take whatever action may be appropriate or necessary in their own countries to eliminate the militarisation of children.
>
> This concern has been brought before us during the International Year of the Child which was proclaimed by the United Nations. We believe that the United Nations is the proper forum for the adoption of agreed measures against the

Child Soldiers

Around the world hundreds of thousands of children – mostly between the ages of 10 and 18, but some as young as 7 years old – are involved in fighting in international wars, civil wars and other situations of militarised violence. Some are legally recruited into government armed forces, such as the 16 and 17-year-olds in the British armed forces. Until 2002, Britain routinely sent under-18s into combat. This changed as a result of the Optional Protocol to the Convention on the Rights of the Child on Involvement of Children in Armed Conflict. Similarly, legal conscription (compulsory service in government armed forces) of under-18s has been nearly eliminated.

However, much illegal recruitment of children continues: into government armed forces, into government-aligned militias or paramilitary forces, and into armed opposition groups. The forces driving such recruitment include:

– the longstanding nature of many of today's conflicts which lead to the death and injury of adult soldiers thus driving down recruitment ages;
– civil wars in particular, which disrupt the life of the community leaving children out of school, orphaned or separated from their families, in need of protection and of the means of survival, thus making them vulnerable to recruitment;
– the development of lightweight, easy to operate, automatic weapons, enabling children, even young ones, to be effective fighters;
– the recognition that children can be persuaded and indoctrinated into killing and committing atrocities once their inhibitions have been broken (by making them kill family members or other children, and with the use of drugs, alcohol and/or adult "leadership" and approval, and threats of death).

Because the worst abuses and youngest ages of child soldiers are associated with long-running civil wars, the issue is perceived as being primarily an African problem. However, because of the size of populations and hence of armed forces, in sheer numbers there are probably more child soldiers in Asia than in Africa, and of course Latin America and other regions are also affected. The most widely quoted statistic – 300,000 child soldiers – was only meant to indicate the numbers likely to be involved in actual combat at any one time, and not to include those in peacetime armed forces. Moreover, all such numbers are inaccurate since the size of the under-18 population in anything but the most organised and open of armed forces is unknowable, and in any case the

number detracts from the understanding of the scope of the problem because it cannot indicate how many people have been recruited and fought as children, since many adult soldiers started in this way, others have been invalided out, or killed, and only a small proportion are actually demobilised whilst they are still under 18. Furthermore, the effects of child soldiering continue even once the conflict, or their involvement in it, has ended.

participation of children in military training and action, and ask our Quaker United Nations Offices to pursue this concern.

This was, therefore, both the origin of the concern and its processing through the orthodox Quaker structures – from the individual, through the monthly meeting, quarterly meeting, yearly meeting and thence to the FWCC Triennial. Since the Triennial happened to be meeting that year and in Switzerland, the progress was remarkably quick. The Triennial clearly put a request to the Quaker UN Offices to work on it, and QUNO Geneva has done so to a greater or lesser extent ever since. In this context, it is important to recall that QUNO represents Friends World Committee for Consultation (FWCC) at the UN, although it is administered and predominantly funded by Britain Yearly Meeting. FWCC as our most broadly representative decision-making body and the sponsor of the Quaker UN work, has some right to lay work on QUNO. It is, in fact, FWCC which has the consultative status with the UN Economic and Social Council, which is what enables QUNO to attend UN meetings, address some UN bodies and make written submissions to them. Thus this was not simply a request from any Quaker body. Equally, QUNO has reported back to FWCC Triennials specifically on this work in addition to its regular reports to the Triennials.

However, child soldiers also remained a personal concern for Dorothea Woods, in which she continued to be supported by Geneva Monthly Meeting (in particular, its Social Concerns Committee). Having started the ball rolling she did not leave it at that but continued to work on the issue. For many years she compiled information into little bulletins entitled "Children Bearing Arms". These comprised extracts and summaries of information she had come across, both in newspapers and on radio or TV, and historical examples from books. As these were distributed and her interest became known, people not only received her bulletins but also sent her information. In addition, she produced some thematic papers to bring out different aspects. QUNO used her work as the basis for its earliest child soldier publications. Subsequently, this compiling and distribution of information was handed over to Rädda Barnen (Swedish Save the Children) who produced an electronic database.

Dorothea herself had typed and reproduced everything manually, in the pre-electronic communication fashion. Although as the years went by Dorothea's own involvement began to lessen, she never lost her "concern" and shortly before her death she wrote to QUNO expressing her thanks for all its work, and in particular for the conclusion and adoption of the Optional Protocol to the Convention on the Rights of the Child on Involvement of Children in Armed Conflict.

This is an interesting example showing that having a personal concern endorsed and adopted as a corporate piece of work does not relieve the individual of their own concern but rather supplements and validates it.

QUNO's role: the facts

In brief, QUNO set to work to try and raise consciousness about the issue and to create international standards to prohibit the military recruitment of children and their use in armed conflicts. In order to do so, QUNO first participated in the drafting of the Convention on the Rights of the Child. In so doing, it achieved the success of having a provision on military use of children included in the Convention* (adopted in 1989), but failed to gain agreement that the prohibition on this use of children should apply to all children as defined in the Convention for all other purposes, in other words, all those up to the age of 18 years. The Convention only prohibited the military recruitment and use in hostilities of those under 15 years (the same age as in the Additional Protocols to the Geneva Conventions adopted in 1977: however, the Additional Protocols do not specify a general age for the limit of "childhood").

In the light of this failure in relation to the Convention on the Rights of the Child, QUNO then persuaded the Committee on the Rights of the Child (the expert body established by the Convention) to devote its first day of discussion to the topic of "Children and Armed Conflict", and recommended that there should be an Optional Protocol to the Convention to remedy its weakness in this respect, and that the Committee should ask for an Expert Study on the subject by the

---

* Article 38.

United Nations Secretary-General. The Committee endorsed both recommendations. The Expert Study became the UN Study on the Impact of Armed Conflict on Children (the Machel Study), for which QUNO was commissioned to do the research on child soldiers.* QUNO was also heavily engaged in the whole of the drafting process for the Optional Protocol from start to finish, including putting forward actual proposals, commenting on those from others, seeking to engage governments positively, and to bring other nongovernmental organisations (NGOs) on board. When the process became stuck (in 1998), QUNO picked up an idea originally proposed by Graça Machel and suggested to the other NGOs the formation of the Coalition to Stop the Use of Child Soldiers, on whose steering committee QUNO still serves.†

However, both during and after the adoption of the Optional Protocol, QUNO also constantly sought other ways of taking the issue forward, in particular through the International Conferences of the Red Cross and Red Crescent Movement, through the International Labour Organisation (ILO), and through research on particular aspects of the problem such as girl soldiers (Yvonne E Keairns 2002, 2003), and why adolescents volunteer (Rachel Brett & Irma Specht 2004).

Why Quakers?

From Dorothea Woods' own explanation, the fact that it was Quakers who saw and took up this issue is logical. Both of the books which Dorothea cites as being the wake-up call for her bring out many aspects of the suffering of children. It was, therefore, she herself who picked out from these different issues the particular topic of children bearing arms and being given military training. Quakers' principled objection to militarisation and the use of military force by anyone might be expected to make them more alert to the particular impact on children of such involvement. As so often with Quakers, this was not universally true as reactions from Friends in different countries

---

* The full version of QUNO's research was published as Rachel Brett & Margaret McCallin: *Children the Invisible Soldiers* (1996).
† For more information on the Coalition, and on the subject of child soldiers, see the Coalition's website: www.child-soldiers.org.

demonstrated. Some Friends did not believe there was any valid distinction between the use of adults and children and thus Quakers should not be working to stop children being recruited, but only to stop all recruitment. Other Friends were willing to consider that there was a problem about young children in "Third World" countries being sent to fight, but that there was nothing wrong with 15 or 16-year-old school leavers in Britain being encouraged to join the armed forces and sent into combat. This is reminiscent of the experience of John Woolman in relation to slavery. The insight and concern of one Friend may come to be adopted by the Society of Friends as a body, but there may be resistance to this and individual Friends may not – at least initially – personally accept the validity of the concern.

Nevertheless, it seems clear that Dorothea did identify a genuine Quaker insight: of course as Quakers we oppose the creation of armed forces and military training for everyone. However, in understanding that children are in need of additional protection precisely because they are children, that is persons who are not yet fully formed physically, mentally and emotionally, she recognised the particularly pernicious effect of subjecting children to military training, attitudes and participation in combat – training for and participating in killing and injuring others in addition to facing death and injury themselves. She also recognised that this is a universal truth – not subject to geography, race, colour, religion, nationality or stage of "development" of their country.

How did being a Quaker concern affect the way in which QUNO worked on the child soldier issue?

Throughout, QUNO has sought to remain true to the underlying concern and the rationale for the concern. That is, as explained above, while continuing to oppose all use of and involvement with military force, in this work focussing on the reasons why we should particularly seek to protect children from such involvement. In that sense, QUNO was seeking to implement a prophetic vision through international law and the bodies established to promote and oversee it. The brief statement of facts of "what QUNO did" set out above could be a presentation by many NGOs working on an issue at the United Nations. In itself it is only really remarkable because QUNO was prepared to continue to work on the issue over a period of years, rather than during a limited campaign timescale and at times with little apparent hope of success. At one point, a diplomat commented despairingly, "We've been working on this for three years", to which our quiet riposte was, "We've been working on it for *eighteen*."

Changing perceptions

In the negotiations at the UN, one of the main arguments was whether under-18s should be excluded from armed forces or whether it was all right for 17-year-olds, or 16-year-olds or 15-year-olds to be involved. QUNO's role was not to provide a definition of who is a child, but to simply keep pointing out that the international community had already decided that it would define a child in legal terms as anyone up to the age of 18. All we asked was that they be consistent in applying this definition and thus that this was also the definition of a child for the purposes of exclusion from armed forces and participation in combat. In other words, the military and "defence" should be treated the same and not differently from other areas of life. As one diplomat whose government was opposing what we were trying to achieve commented in disbelief after repeatedly having tried to persuade QUNO that there was really no difference between 17 and 18 years as the applicable age, "You mean it's a matter of principle!"

This insistence on consistent application of international standards combined with its radical understanding of the issues and refusal to accept traditional compartmentalisation, was also at the root of QUNO's ultimately successful efforts to get child soldiering identified as a form of child labour. Previously, the armed forces had been exempted from this area of international law. As a result of QUNO's insight and activities, not only did the International Labour Organisation (ILO) Worst Forms of Child Labour Convention (No 182) specifically prohibit "forced labour, including forced or compulsory recruitment of children for use in armed conflict" (children being defined as all those under 18 years), but in the light of this, the ILO itself went back and reinterpreted the earlier Convention on Minimum Age for Employment (No 138) as also covering military recruitment and use in armed conflict, which it had previously considered to be excluded from the provisions of this Convention.

To summarise: QUNO consistently sought to change people's (and through them governments' and international organisations') understanding, and therefore attitudes, not merely to impose an apparently arbitrary legal standard in relation to the issue of "child soldiering". Many could not understand why we wasted so much time on what they thought was a trivial issue. Only a few of the people involved in the processes understood the real nature of the conceptual change QUNO was trying to achieve and the enormity of the task. One perceptive diplomat, near the conclusion of the negotiations on the Optional Protocol, commented quietly, "Don't underestimate what you have achieved. I think we will look back on this as a historic moment: the first time the armed forces have been regulated by way of a human rights treaty."

Methodology

Because QUNO was seeking to effect change for the purpose of effecting change, it sought always to find and encourage allies rather than to ward off "trespassers" and claim this as "our issue". Similarly QUNO was not concerned to advertise its role, being happy to share successes with others – both governmental and nongovernmental. This is in line with QUNO's general method of working on issues, but it is important to see how this shaped the strategy on this one. Thus QUNO deliberately and proactively worked to bring in other NGOs, in particular those larger, with more weight, lobbying power and different skills from its own, such as Human Rights Watch and Amnesty International, without fearing that they might take over the issue and get credit which "should" be QUNO's. The quality of the relationship built amongst the NGOs involved in the Coalition was strong enough to withstand the efforts of the opposed governments to create disunity, and even in the face of what the NGOs considered failure in relation to the Optional Protocol, there was no falling out or laying of blame amongst them, and this continues to be the case.

In the same way, the quality of the relationship established with many government representatives – and not only those on "our side" – was such that real mutual respect and friendship developed. Indeed, an extraordinary tribute to QUNO's perceived expertise, integrity and even-handed ability to listen to all parties was the way that on one of the most sensitive issues, that of recruitment and use of children by armed groups, QUNO was not only specifically asked to join the intergovernmental informal negotiations, but ended up facilitating the penultimate round of them which produced the formula which formed the basis for the final agreement on this provision.

For QUNO, one of the frustrations has been the way in which the media, some governments and others tended to "hijack" the issue, presenting it in ways which did not reflect the full understanding of the reality and the concept encompassed in the Quaker insight. Thus, too often, the refrains were about "abducted children", about "10-year-olds in Africa" and about girls being used for sexual purposes. Both QUNO's research and the Quaker understanding of the issue clearly identified the problems: all children should be included (as defined by the international standards, so up to the age of 18 years), from whatever region of the world (so under-18s in the UK should receive the same protection as African children), whether they were physically forced to join or were encouraged/persuaded/ indoctrinated to do so or really volunteered (since the effects of militarisation and participation do not change because of the method of becoming involved); and it should be recognised that girls fight – in addition to multi-tasking (cooking, portering, providing first aid, and yes, providing "sexual services") as women and girls do in other walks of life. This is why QUNO has continued to identify and undertake, or encourage others to undertake, additional research and advocacy to constantly restore the centrality of the underlying Quaker insight and concern.

Of course QUNO did not always live up to its intentions. There were times when we became too much of an advocate – too confrontational – and thus perhaps lost our ability to persuade those who did not agree with us. Many mistakes were undoubtedly made too, but the benefit of actually working to change perceptions rather than just outward behaviour is that inward change lasts. The moment in which it became clear to me that we had really made an impact was at the European Conference to Stop the Use of Child Soldiers, organised by the Child Soldiers Coalition in Berlin in October 1999. Sitting on the podium, I realised that, apart from the UK, no European government was any longer suggesting that there was nothing wrong with sending under-18s into combat. This had certainly not been the case when I joined QUNO in 1993.

Corporate or personal concern?

When I first started working at QUNO, child soldiers was one of the priority issues I inherited. It was only as I became more involved in it personally, undertaking research and meeting former child soldiers and their families, that I came to understand what was happening and its impact, and then to realise that I could no longer simply say that this was one of the issues on which I worked. In that sense, the corporate concern also became a personal one for me: not something that I could take or leave; not something that at the end of the working day I could simply switch off and forget about. My family can amply testify the way in which the issue invaded our family life. My children once commented that in that particular year they could not recall a single family meal at which child soldiers had not been discussed! Two of my predecessors at QUNO Geneva are still involved with the child soldier issue too! Is this, perhaps, a hallmark of a real Quaker concern, that even when integrated into the "central work", those working on it became engaged in it personally?

Laying down a personal/corporate concern

The problem arises for this kind of work of when to stop doing it. Given the small size of QUNO and the constant requests and needs for other issues to be taken up at the UN, do we at some point decide that we have fulfilled the calling to work on child soldiers? If so, who decides and on what basis? This again relates to the nature of the substantive concern: if the objective set for QUNO was to get an Optional Protocol to the Convention on the Rights of the Child, then logically the adoption of this Protocol should have ended QUNO's involvement. But the Protocol does not prohibit all recruitment and use of under-18s, so is QUNO bound to continue to try to achieve that result? Equally, as outlined above, despite the Protocol not only are children still being recruited and sent into combat, but some of the insights – about adolescent volunteers, about girl soldiers, and so on – could only begin to be picked up once QUNO resources were freed from the major work to obtain the Protocol. Furthermore, the original concern also included the military training of children – an area that QUNO has barely touched because so much time and energy had to be devoted to trying to get the prohibition on actual recruitment and participation in hostilities. Finally, there is the question of the expectation of others and the expertise that QUNO has gained on the issue. Despite getting so many others "on board" and actively engaged in the child soldier issue, QUNO is still seen as a resource and major player.

In the case of a personal Quaker concern, there is an inevitable time limit: either the individual senses that the concern has been fulfilled or death intervenes. For a corporate concern, some form of discernment process is needed to establish whether the concern has been accomplished or perhaps that the involvement of the central bodies is no longer required. Such a decision need not, of course, preclude individual Quakers from pursuing the matter whether directly as Quakers or through other organisations. In this way, the process can come full circle, from the individual, through the Quaker processes and structures, and back to the individual.

Chapter 7

Speaking Truth to the International Financial Institutions

by Robin Robison

Nicaragua has suffered greatly in the last twenty-five years and has been in many ways the victim of neo-colonialism by the United States from the very early part of the twentieth century till today. It is not possible to understand the current situation there without some knowledge of the history of the country, particularly since the fall of the Somoza regime in the late 1970s. Nicaragua is a post-conflict country and its politics and economic situation are still deeply affected by the conflict there in the 1980s. Many individuals are traumatised, and a fractured political system makes governance at times almost impossible. The American Friends Service Committee (AFSC) has had a programme there for many years, in which staff presence and support for grass roots movements resulted in a deep understanding of the political and cultural context in which present conflicts were played out. In the 1980s AFSC supported and funded community building and reconciliation work to try and help the situation created by the conflict between the government and the rebels funded by the USA. Also AFSC has been continually engaged in lobbying work in Washington in relation to Nicaragua and other Central American countries on behalf of a large number of campaigning groups and social movements from all parts of the country. Although Quaker Peace & Service had in the 1980s and early 1990s a Latin American Programme this was not the reason why its successor Quaker Peace & Social Witness (QPSW) decided to begin working with AFSC in Nicaragua. This article will set out some of the wider perspective in Nicaragua, both politically and economically, as well as explaining why QPSW engaged in joint work there with AFSC.

Nicaragua, like most poor countries, is deeply in debt to the International Monetary Fund (IMF), and the World Bank – institutions that are dominated by the Western powers and that do not have anything like adequate lines of accountability running from the decision making at the top in Washington or in various European capitals to the faraway people most affected by their policy decisions.* Notoriously the Bank and Fund have a reputation of walking into developing countries with "structural adjustment plans"; these are ready made economic blueprints, designed in Washington, and then imposed on a developing country without any consultation with those who live there apart from a few officials in the Finance Ministry. Interest rates imposed by the IMF and World Bank have been low, but nevertheless a severe burden on small economies. The institutions operate for the most part on a revolving fund basis, not a profitmaking basis. This means that they insist that the money lent comes back in a timely manner in order that it can be loaned out again to someone else.

Developing countries have to agree to certain responsibilities that come with the financial loans from the IMF and World Bank. Some of these responsibilities are to be expected – such as ensuring that the money is used for the purpose for which it was loaned and that interest and capital payments are made in a timely manner. However, the economic approach of the international financial institutions has been dominated by what is known as the neo-liberal school of thought, and there is a tendency for the international financial institutions to be used by the G7 countries as vehicles for their foreign policy. The result is an institutional bias in favour of private ownership and control rather than public management; the international institutions also demand open markets for free access by privately controlled capital and companies, meaning in practice the capital and companies from Europe and the USA.

All the principal lines of credit in the Bank and Fund have processes tied to them in which applicant countries have to participate fully in order to qualify for concessionary interest rates and repayment timing on their borrowing. Their governments have to agree to implement reforms which have included privatisation of public utilities, tight fiscal targets and increasing their international reserves,

---

* The World Bank and International Monetary Fund are run by executive boards whose members are appointed by their respective governments. Each country has power on the board proportionate to its financial contribution to the Fund; so countries like the UK and France have huge power, whereas countries like Mozambique have very little.

as well as legal reforms to judicial processes and banking practices. On their own in a neutral context some of these reforms are desirable. However problems are caused by the lack of democracy and absence of true consultation between the governments and the international institutions. There is no question that dogma is also a problem, as there has been unwavering faith amongst many of the staff in the IMF and World Bank that the neo-liberal or "Chicago school" of economic thinking with its emphasis on market forces and privatisation is the only valid way for countries to go. Fundamentally this is a question of "Do as I say, not do as I did", as historically the American and European economies developed along lines totally at odds with what is being imposed on the current "developing world".

It needs to be remembered that the reason many of the developing countries had to approach the IMF in the first place was because of balance of payments difficulties. In other words the country's overall economic situation was not sustainable, and the trade situation in particular was bad, leading to its fiscal problems. But the country had no way of increasing its income to repay the institutions that had lent it money. It also needs to be remembered that such countries are not just facing external debt from these two institutions but also commercial debt from banks overseas as well as internal debts to private banks and individuals. Often the internal debts are held at much higher interest rates than the debts to the multilateral institutions, and on much shorter repayment terms.*

Dramatic fluctuations in commodity prices have been an important additional cause of serious economic problems, especially in countries like Nicaragua which are largely dependent on a few vulnerable commodities like coffee.

In the 1990s, British Friends established a dialogue with the International Monetary Fund, the World Bank and also the Bank of

---

* Internal debt is debt incurred by the government to commercial banks and wealthy individuals within the country in order to access credit for a variety of purposes. Highly Indebted Poor Countries (HIPC) are not allowed to access the international money markets, principally New York and London, and therefore have to turn to other sources of funds, often at higher rates than International Monetary Fund and World Bank loans. Internal debt does not qualify for HIPC relief and so has to be dealt with by the government outside any international assistance agreements.

England and the UK Treasury and some representatives of merchant banks in the City of London. The main aim of this work was to create and keep open a channel of communication with institutions that are very powerful in the developing world. This dialogue, like most recent Quaker diplomatic work, was not done with a view to achieving specific objectives but the result was that over time a small number of staff in the institutions, particularly in the IMF, became sympathetic to the Quaker voice and perceived that we had no axe to grind and that our only real objective in this work was to be a facilitator. After the departmental changes in Britain Yearly Meeting in 2002, the new Economic Issues Group of Quaker Peace & Social Witness (QPSW) looked for ways to continue this dialogue.

On the other side of the Atlantic the AFSC had a quite different approach to the continued expansion of a global free market economy. In this period there was a very lively antiglobalisation movement developing across the world which made its presence felt at gatherings of policy makers and politicians for discussion and decision making. AFSC had stayed in the streets and had played a prominent role in the protest movements around the United States at the local and state level, as well as at the national and international levels.

QPSW had not stayed out of the streets – indeed its Turning the Tide programme had trained antiglobalisation groups in nonviolent direct action – but the key difference lay in a different view of the institutions. Essentially AFSC believed that the financial institutions must be torn down, while QPSW believed that the institutions needed reform in order to make them begin to reflect the needs of the poorest people in the countries with IMF and World Bank programmes. As the staff member directly engaged with the work with the institutions and in discussions with the AFSC staff I was very aware of the tensions between the different approaches to the problems presented by globalisation, but equally I could see that essentially our Quaker values were the same and we wanted the same outcome. It was in such discussions in the Quaker United Nations Office (QUNO) in Geneva with AFSC staff that I began to see the possibility of a mutually beneficial joining together of AFSC and QPSW work. The Geneva connection grew in importance over time as it became clear that in order to address the situation as a whole we must consider the impact of multilateral trade negotiations mediated through the World Trade Organisation and also regional trade negotiations, for example the Central American Free Trade Agreement. We ended up with a three-way Quaker conversation, between AFSC, QPSW and QUNO Geneva, all assisting each other from their expertise. QUNO Geneva was able to bring in trade experts from Geneva when dialogue meetings were held in Nicaragua, thus making a distinctive contribution of its own.

In this ad hoc and informal way an idea was born which was then tested in committee. Serving Quaker committees for over fourteen years, including for this specific project, has shown me that mutual trust between staff and committee members is essential for the process to work well, and in my experience this has almost always been the case. The interactions that took place in order to arrive at committee decisions relating to our work in Nicaragua were more complex than usual as they included both AFSC and QUNO Geneva. Like all Quaker business meetings, committees at Friends House use Quaker worship and Quaker minuting techniques. As with any meetings, the committees at the corporate level sometimes work well and sometimes less well, depending on the mix of personalities in the group at the time. In our work with AFSC in Nicaragua the key decision maker was the Economic Issues Group, with QPSW Central Committee only having the role of reviewing the work, and with Meeting for Sufferings approving extra-budgetary funding.

Committee members have the crucial task of ensuring that the decision is taken in the Quaker way as well as adhering to the Quaker testimonies and the terms of reference agreed by Central Committee. Certainly the experience of this work has demonstrated that unity is required rather than unanimity and that this is the basis of Quaker decision-making, not consensus. It is very hard to identify in which way such centrally planned Quaker work is Spirit-led, as there is less of a community focal point for the worship-based decision-making than is generally found in local Quaker meetings. Nevertheless I have no doubt that this project, with its strong connections to grassroots groups in Nicaragua, was Spirit-led and in keeping with the values of Friends in Britain Yearly Meeting, as it has strengthened those groups and also opened doors with what had seemed monolithic institutions.

The role of staff is a complex one which has been evolving over the last decade. The Spirit can certainly work through staff, whether Quakers or not, and through committee members and in any number of creative interactions and synergies between them. Quaker processes are an essential part of the business in decision-making, but so is detailed knowledge of policies and situation. My experience in this work has been that staff bring the detailed knowledge and committee Friends bring discernment and thinking which is then combined with the detailed knowledge. The two together are what is put into the Quaker business meeting, out of which comes a piece of Quaker work which we hope will further the aims of the yearly meeting and of the Spirit in the world.

Nicaragua as one recipient of assistance programmes of the IMF and World Bank was an obvious starting point. Because of AFSC's long-term presence in there and their deep connections with and understanding of its civil society groups, they had an appreciation for the difficulties caused by the international institutions to the majority of the people. Conversely QPSW had developed a good working knowledge of the IMF and World Bank, and because of the dialogue work already carried out, there was a sympathetic ear in Washington to listen to our concerns about the country. Each Quaker institution had been working at a different end of the same problem and it was a case of putting them together in a way that was mutually beneficial and resulted in higher quality work being done in Nicaragua.

The majority of people in Nicaragua live on under two dollars a day, with poverty in the rural areas being particularly severe. The country is dependent on a few crops to earn their foreign income (coffee and sesame seeds) and some manufacturing in export processing zones dominated by Korean multinational companies. Because of the high level of external debts Nicaragua is one of the Highly Indebted Poor Countries (HIPC) in the world. As in all the other HIPC countries, Nicaragua has been subjected to a Poverty Reduction Strategy Paper (PRSP) process by the IMF and World Bank. These are the successors to the "structural adjustment programmes" already mentioned; but the theory behind PRSPs is much better, in that they are supposed to be designed by the country applying for the assistance, with civil society input as well as government, and then agreed by the boards of the Fund and Bank in Washington. The reality is, as one might expect, more complex than the theory. Experience in Nicaragua demonstrates how difficult it is to design national economic plans in a genuinely participative way with people from all sections of society.

The difficulty with the implementation of the PRSP process in Nicaragua (and throughout the highly indebted poor countries) underlines the problem with the lack of transparency in the international financial institutions and their governance. These powerful institutions are a sixty-year-old legacy of the end of the Second World War and reflect the world order and power relations at that time, not the world as it is now – in particular the way in which the vast majority of the world's populations have to live under the dictates of the most wealthy but least populous countries in the world. Although colonialism formally ended in the 1960s, for very many countries it has lived on in all but name, only this time the enforcing authorities are the IMF and the World Bank. This has been most thoroughly demonstrated in the way that economic policy has been essentially forced down the throats of developing countries.

From the Quaker perspective, work on economic justice arises from the Quaker testimony to simplicity and also the testimony to equality. We say it is quite wrong that the majority of the world's population are forced to live on so little when a minority of people (almost all in Europe and the United States) live in comparative luxury with considerable power to determine the future of the majority. Historically Friends have been concerned with issues relating to peace. An unjust way of life contributes to tensions that can lead to conflict and war. In this way issues of simplicity, justice and peace are all linked.

In order to address these fundamental issues Friends have worked on their own and with others seeking to alleviate suffering and change the world in ways that will lead eventually to a fairer distribution of the world's resources without contributing to lingering resentments. As yet there is no unity in Britain Yearly Meeting about what kind of economic system best serves the aims to which we aspire, but we are united in believing that structures need to serve human needs rather than the other way round. It is with this in mind that both the QPSW Economic Issues Group and Quaker United Nations Office have worked to reform policy makers' thinking in the principal international financial institutions. Although it was possible to engage policy makers in discussions about general issues of concern, it proved much more effective to be specific from experience in depth in one country which could, to some degree, serve as an example for many other countries in a similar situation. Co-ordinating with AFSC and making use of their knowledge of civil society in Nicaragua enabled QPSW to do just this.

Working in the way described achieved more than gaining credibility with the institutions. Crucially it also allowed AFSC and QPSW to give a voice to civil society in Nicaragua and therefore to those with least power but who are most affected by decisions made over their heads. Until recently civil society had little in the way of direct contact with international institutions regarding the design of poverty reduction plans. Within both the IMF and the World Bank we have discovered that one must discuss country-specific issues with those officials who have direct responsibility for negotiations between the institutions and the relevant governments. So in this case we have been meeting with the Nicaragua mission chief from the Fund and the senior adviser to the Board in the Bank. Such meetings are friendly but also time-pressured and there is always a need to make sure that the main issues concerning us are aired and addressed by the officials present. It is not the top level officials with wider responsibilities who need to be addressed on such detailed issues but staff with a good knowledge of the in-country problems, politics and peculiarities.

We are not trying on these occasions to put forward a northern groups' agenda; our main aim has been to try and make sure that Nicaraguan views have been conveyed to the institutions. Our main way of doing this has been to bring Nicaraguan economists to the IMF and World Bank and facilitate an exchange of views. AFSC staff and I were always present at these meetings in the institutions, and the information from the Nicaraguan contacts was conveyed directly by them to the officials in the meetings. Sometimes too, after meetings in Managua with contacts there, I would call in at the institutions on the way back from Nicaragua to London and make use of being on the western side of the Atlantic.

Although there had certainly been officially organised meetings during the design of the Poverty Reduction Strategy Paper, which the

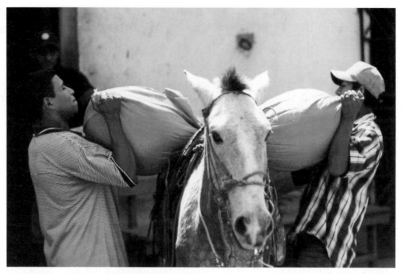

Nicaraguan coffee co-operative

IMF and World Bank asked for, it became clear in discussion with the civil society groups that this consultation process had been a skin-deep exercise which did not extend to groups outside the capital city or to many dissenting voices in groups with alternative policy approaches. By our work, QPSW and AFSC have been able to allow civil society voices to be aired inside the institutions. We enabled civil society representatives and Nicaraguan economists to visit the IMF and World Bank and they were able to raise well-grounded concerns with the officials who have week-by-week responsibility for making decisions about loans and other programmes in Nicaragua. These meetings have carried on and are still taking place as I write in mid 2005. Opportunities have continued to arise which allow us to make a direct input to official thinking. We also communicate with the UK delegation in Washington, who have been able to use the information at IMF and World Bank board discussions.

Principal topics of our conversations with the institutions have related to the Highly Indebted Poor Countries programme and how this has worked for Nicaragua, and the conditions attached to the loans from the IMF and the World Bank, as well as the Inter-American Development Bank. The methodology has included research commissioned by QPSW and AFSC from Nicaraguan economists which takes a critical look at the Bank and Fund programmes; this is then used as the basis for the dialogue with the institutions. In summary three main problems have been identified in this way.

1. Although the theory of debt write-off by the international community under the HIPC programme sounds promising, the experience in Nicaragua has been that a significant proportion of funds released from debt service in the national budget have not appeared in expenditure on poverty reduction programmes but have been used to fund service on internal debt that has been built up over the last few years.* The problem is that the interest rate and repayment arrangements for this type of debt has been undermining development programmes. Since the IMF interferes in the Nicaraguan economy in so many other ways, we raised with the IMF the need for them to also ensure that interest rates for the internal debt were set at a level which allowed the funds available for development to expand. In this way they could be consistent about their interference in developing country economies.

2. The conditions attached to the IMF and World Bank programmes have been damaging for Nicaragua. In particular the privatisation of water and electricity damages the poorest in the community who have least ability to pay for these essential services. The key condition imposed by the institutions has been to charge the full costs of services, and of course the private companies who have been allowed by the changes in the law to take control of the water service are not interested in subsidising the poorest people. Seeking a profit is one thing in a wealthy country like the UK but quite another in a country where most people are living on under two dollars per day and many on much less than that. Needless to say, this policy causes divisions in Nicaraguan society. It isn't yet clear what the result of the stand-off between the government and others will be.

---

* Evidence from research commissioned by Quaker Peace & Social Witness and American Friends Service Committee has shown that in Nicaragua over $100 million from funds released from debt relief under the Heavily Indebted Poor Countries initiative was used by the government to service its huge levels of internal debt.

3. The IMF insists that Nicaragua gives priority to building up financial reserves in the Nicaraguan central bank. This takes away from expenditure on essential services like health and education.

Since these dialogue meetings, the team from the IMF dealing with Nicaragua has met on a number of occasions with civil society representatives in Managua independent from QPSW and AFSC. Such meetings had not happened before. Nicaraguan civil society representatives tell us that the facilitation of these meetings with the IMF and World Bank which includes them has been very useful and has empowered them, making them feel less the victims of powers entirely outside their influence.

Policy work which has no direct relationship to actual grassroots experiences risks being patronising towards the very people it is purporting to help; while campaigning without policy work fails to connect with the international financial institutions and influence them. By joining up the work of AFSC, QPSW and QUNO we have shown that Friends can work both for detailed policy change and for change of the whole system to better reflect the world it is meant to be serving.

Chapter 8
Faith and Practice
Believing, Acting and Witnessing
by Diana Francis

This book is an account of the ways in which different Friends have tried to work in the spirit of our faith and testimonies. In my life in the field of conflict transformation (Diana Francis 2002), I have met and worked with many people, of different faiths and no named faith, who work in the same spirit. That is one of the things that gives me hope in spite of the many reasons for despair: that this work is growing and that so many courageous and committed people are giving their lives to building peace, even in the most dangerous and desperate of places.

Brian Phillips's account, in his opening chapter, of the sense of recognition between Friends and fellow peaceworkers in the former Yugoslavia, when they came to talk about the spirit underlying their work, was heartwarming and came as no surprise. Whatever the language used to describe it, this for me is "that of God" in operation: what early Friends also called "the spirit of Christ".

Chris Lawson (a former Senior Tutor at Woodbrooke) came to speak to my local meeting, recently, about the worldwide family of Friends. He named the things that, in spite of all our differences, bound us to one another: the centrality of personal spiritual experience; the collective experience of the worshipping group; our insistence on the inseparability of faith and practice; and our belief in the sacredness of all life. This last, fundamental belief is expressed in our testimonies, particularly our peace testimony, which is at the heart of our Quaker identity – both the way we understand ourselves and the way others see us. What I want to do in this chapter is to make a rallying call to Friends to make sure we keep it so. In so doing I will pick up on Grigor McClelland's theme of "prophets and reconcilers" (finding myself in both camps) and identify some other polarities that we experience as a Society. I will argue that, in spite of all our doubts, faith can be our most important contribution to the healing of our world.

For now, let me continue with Chris Lawson, who divided the peace testimony into two parts: conscientious objection and mission. Since we have no conscription in this country, our objection must of necessity be broader, aimed at war policies and acts of war for which our government is responsible. Our mission can be understood in two ways: going to work with others to help them achieve peace, and going out to witness or testify to others in our own society, at whatever level, about the need to prevent or abolish war and build peace in its place. Several of those who have contributed to this book are involved in mission in the former sense, working with others to transform their situations. Most Friends are not directly involved in such work, though they are glad to know that it is being done. Rachel Brett and Robin Robison have described work that is aimed at changing policy and some of us may have had some involvement in supporting campaigns for such policy changes. In any case, we are all involved, as citizens, in what is done in the world, at home and abroad, by our governments in our name. Our primary responsibility as citizens is to do all in our power to elect and persuade our political representatives to act in favour of the values we hold for society.

Ours is a country that advocates "peaceful resolution" for others but is shockingly ready to use large scale military violence in pursuit of its own goals. It finds billions of pounds for wars that destroy people, economies and environments, while fundamental human needs remain unmet in large parts of the world. How do we, as Friends, "testify" in this situation? I would argue that protest against particular wars is not enough. The testimony that we have developed as Friends is against war as such. I believe it is that radical testimony that is needed today.

It was that radical testimony that first drew me to Quakers. I grew up in the Congregational Church. Although Friends, to my chagrin, tend to use the word "congregationalism" somewhat pejoratively (as in "creeping congregationalism"), I experienced the Congregational Church of those days as non-doctrinaire, Spirit-led and committed to the practical living of faith. Most of its members did not, however, share my parents' belief that the teachings, life and death of Jesus all pointed to the unconditional rejection of war and violence. Their convictions, their history as conscientious objectors and their continuing involvement in the peace movement were respected by most and tolerated by all, but not shared. I accepted this, but was at a loss to imagine what our fellow worshippers saw as the "good news", if they thought there was no way out of the cruelty and destructiveness of current ways of doing things. How did they understand Jesus' teaching: as exaggerating for the sake of effect – therefore manipulative and cynical – or just plain wrong, deluded? And how did they see his death: as an unmitigated disaster, the outcome of folly – showing what happens to agitators who get their analysis wrong? Yet it was held to be the centre of our faith, and the phrase "take up your cross" was often used.

I loved my old church and am still grateful for all it taught and gave me. But I gravitated to the Society of Friends because for me this was such a hole in the church's life and witness that it left me feeling isolated and unsupported. Among Quakers I would feel "normal". Their historic peace testimony was undisputed. Their central emphasis on "that of God in everyone" was in line with the heart of Jesus' teaching: that each of us is made in God's image, is a child of

15 February 2003

God, whose very hairs are numbered. This was the basis for the call to nonviolence and why Friends rejected war. They were convinced that this spirit of God in us would never allow us to violate or kill another person because, whatever the realities of evil and conflict, we would recognise God in them and know there was another way.

This book is witness to the fact that the peace testimony still finds expression in the lives of many Friends, in a wide variety of ways. And peace is more than the absence of war. It embraces our other testimonies, to truth, justice, equality, simplicity, and care for our planet. But I have come to realise something that would shock non-Friends: that many Quakers are uncomfortable with the peace testimony as it relates to the principled objection to war, feeling that to take a "pacifist" position is simplistic, strident and divisive. And quite a proportion of those who discover the Society and feel at home with the experience of silent worship regard the peace testimony almost as an optional extra – or, when they take it seriously, as a stumbling block. Many Friends are uncomfortable when it is the subject of ministry, and feel oppressed by any assumption that we are united in holding to it.

It is essential that we should be able to be honest with each other. And as a non-credal Society we have no right to "police" each other's convictions. Yet it is strange and uncomfortable that those among us who hold passionately to something so historic and central to our collective identity can be experienced by others as too dogmatic. And what does this mean for our faith – that so many of us do not see Jesus' teaching, or that of our founders, as practicable "in the real world"? Whether we belong to the "Christocentric" or to the "universalist" tendency within the Society, the challenge is the same.

Why has the old unity of conviction deserted us, at a time when it seems that the institution of war has run right out of control; when "weapons of mass destruction" are continuing to spread, just as the old anti-nuclear movement predicted they would, and the nuclear powers are involved in fresh spirals of "vertical proliferation"; when we know that militarism accounted for a hundred million deaths in the last century; when the proportion of civilian deaths in war is rising ever higher; when television brings war's atrocities right into our living rooms; when we know we are squandering a vast proportion of our wealth on the means of death while millions die in want? Surely this is a time when it should be clearer than ever, from a simply human – let alone Quaker – point of view, that war is an abomination?

Faith and action

I believe there are several reasons why what Grigor McClelland has called the "prophetic" aspect of our peace testimony is sometimes experienced in negative ways by Friends. I believe that some of these are related to broader tendencies within our Society that lie behind the prophet/reconciler positions. I think I detect among us a small, endemic and subterranean conflict, between those whose main energy goes into "doing" and those who prefer to see life in terms of "being". In reality the conflict is fictional. Being and doing are part of each other: the life of faith is expressed in the life of practice; and doing nothing is doing something, in that it has an effect.

Yet those of us in the Society who are "activists" can feel they are considered as lacking in spiritual depth, while those who are not can feel the activism of others as a reproach. They counter with the reminder that "peace begins in our hearts". That, in turn, seems to suggest that outward action is an enemy of the inner life. But spirit and action need each other. Seeing faith and practice as one is one of our hallmarks as Friends – or so we would like to think. While some of us may more naturally fit into the contemplative mould and others are more active by nature, it is my experience that these different tendencies can be thoroughly supportive of each other, if their interdependence is acknowledged.

I know several Friends who, unconvinced of the feasibility of rejecting all wars, or uncomfortable with political campaigns, have expressed their faithfulness to the peace testimony by engaging in practical peacemaking not abroad but at home: by promoting peace education in schools, helping set up a neighbourhood mediation service, promoting the notion and practice of restorative justice, or working for good race relations in their town. It can certainly be argued that initiatives like Leicester Friends' work with asylum seekers are far more productive than the apparently futile efforts of campaigners to dent the military machine. This is good, practical peacemaking, important in its own right and a very practical witness to the faith that we hold. I am sure that all Friends feel comfortable with it. I have participated in some of this work and found it enriching and satisfying – a welcome antidote to the frustrations of apparently wasted years in the "peace movement". But its effect on me is not to make me feel that "prophecy" is the less needed. Because it demonstrates so clearly that human relations can be managed so much more constructively than by hate and threat, it gives body to my belief that a world without war is possible. It has only fuelled my belief that war is wrong and unnecessary and my determination that, in spite of everything, alongside my work as a "reconciler", I must go on working for political change and witnessing for the rejection and abolition of war.

If "reconciling" action is found to be acceptable, it is not action per se that is the cause of unease, so where does the problem really lie? The perceived conflict between doing and being overlaps with the tension often felt between the spiritual and the political. Political activism is not only too active but it's the wrong sort of action. To relate this to Grigor McClelland's prophets and reconcilers: the latter may be active, but in a personal way that involves supporting others in doing good things, rather than seeking to change systems through political engagement. Do you remember that quotation from the Brazilian bishop, Dom Helder Camara, who said, "When I gave food to the poor, they called me a saint. When I asked why the poor were hungry, they called me a communist"? I believe that, like him, we must concern ourselves with the systems out of which violent conflicts arise, as well as trying to deal with their effects.

Moreover, some of the conflicts we work with in our "reconciler" role need to be addressed through political structures by politicians, and they in turn need to be challenged and supported by politically active citizens. Reconciliation comes, if at all, at the end of the line, often after processes of mobilisation and confrontation to address violence and injustice. (Think, for example, of South Africa, which is working for reconciliation after years of political struggle.) So the reconciling work is also political and mediators cannot themselves make peace: only the parties to the conflict can do that.

I think that confrontation is felt by some of us to be "unpeaceful". Certainly there is a risk of being aggressive and self-righteous in the way we go about it, and we could adopt, properly and effectively, a more dialogical approach to public action and debate. The spirit of our protest must be consonant with the care and respect that we want to uphold, and when we participate in broad movements and coalitions the context for this may not be easy. Yet I have found that to be faithful in this can be an important and influential form of witness within a movement.

The unease Friends often have about engaging with differences belongs, I feel, with a wider confusion between conflict as such and violence or aggression. They are not the same things. Conflict can be highly constructive and is almost always a necessary part of change. It need harm or dishonour no-one. Feeling uncomfortable is not necessarily bad for us! If peace meant simply the absence of turbulence, the most "peaceful" state we could look forward to would be death.

To stress the need to say no to war is seen in itself, by some, as negative – "bad energy" – especially when it takes the form of public protest. Yet wouldn't a world without war be a wonderful improvement? And aren't we glad that people said no to slavery? Don't we wish that more people had protested against Hitler's policies of genocide? Aren't we glad that torture is outlawed? Don't we think it's important that poverty should be identified as a blot on the human landscape? Isn't it good that people are warning against global pollution? It is often in recognising wrong for what it is that we are able to open the way for what is right. Saying no can be powerfully positive: liberating, life affirming and necessary. Simon Fisher, in his 2004 Swarthmore Lecture, puts this very well:

> In joining with others in conspiring, and then confronting a particular issue or injustice, we both chart out another stretch of our own journey and offer a signpost to others, to respond as they wish.

Clarity in our witness

So far we have been looking at the relationship between faith and practice and at the forms which practice can take. But now we need to go back to faith itself and our calling to "testify" to it. We cannot – and should not – witness to what we do not ourselves believe. And

"Ecumenical Accompanier" (baseball cap) with Palestinian girls in Hebron, at risk of being stoned: this World Council of Churches project is administered in Britain by Quaker Peace & Social Witness

the trouble is that while we see all too clearly what war does, we also see what unopposed violence can do. Many of us feel that if we are to reject war we must have "an answer" to the many and terrible situations of violence that arise around us. The worst thing seems to be to do nothing – even if the alternative is to do something that compounds the disaster and perpetuates the dynamics and the very system of violence.

This logic, or I would say the lack of it, is encouraged by the fact that the media, which present us with the images of cruelty that may persuade us that war is necessary, rarely follow "the story" once the war is over. We see war's destructive aftermath only when, as in Vietnam or Iraq, the violence continues at such a pitch and involves the big powers in such a way that it cannot be hidden. (No-one tells us how grim and dangerous life is now in Kosovo, for instance, and Afghanistan has largely left the news.) And it is all too easy to forget the people whose lives have been snuffed out, whose bodies have been maimed, or whose future has been ruined by the loss of those who were dearest to them. They are soon lost to sight.

We often talk about "alternatives to war", as if we had a system that worked and that we therefore needed to replace. I believe that to be a very powerful and longstanding myth, and in my recent book (Diana Francis 2004) I have tried to deconstruct it, arguing that the reasons given for going to war are seldom the "just causes" that are claimed; that other means are never first exhausted and seldom even tried; and that wars seldom achieve the good things that are purported to be their purpose, while their catastrophic outcomes are all too predictable. I have pointed out that the whole point of militarism is that brute force prevails. It has nothing to do with democracy and is designed not for the protection of the weak but for the dominance of the strong. Even those who believe in it do not see how to use it – or do not do so – in the instances that most exercise us. And even the greatest powers could not militarily quell all the current violent conflicts. I argue that war is the antithesis of human rights and that its preparation and justification undermine the very notion of them. At the same time I acknowledge that our sense of humanity requires us to care for each other and stand up for good against cruelty and injustice. I have pointed to "active nonviolence" as a well demonstrated but insufficiently explored (and resourced) means of doing this, representing "the power of the powerless" and enabling them to stand up for their own rights rather than waiting for military champions.

I wrote this book, in part, to see if what I still believed, in spite and indeed because of my experience of working with violent conflict, was capable of explanation – to myself and to others. I wanted to gather together and examine the inner knowledge that was constantly under assault from a battery of information, disinformation, and the near-overwhelming turbulence and distress of the daily news. I hope the book will help some people and make a small dent in some of the assumptions that need to be changed if the human race is to progress. I believe that until we can persuade ourselves to let go of war as an option and allow ourselves to admit that it is simply morally unacceptable – like torture and slavery – we will not be able to move forward: to release our spirit, intellect and ingenuity to develop the ideas and systems that can bring a real increase in human security, respect and compassion.

Other Friends will believe that all these systems need to be in place, at least conceptually, before we can make the break. What we are looking at is in any case a process: one that cannot be predicted but must be entered into by all of us in our own ways. Somehow we need to get from the world where we are to the world where we want to be. I believe that faith is the bridge between the two and can help us cope with the uncertainty inherent in stepping into the unknown. Not only does it give us the positive energy we need to make the leap, the vision without which our nightmares are likely to become self-fulfilling prophecies; it also provides the existential grounding for our hope and action. The belief that human beings, however depraved, have the capacity for good and therefore are both worthy of respect and capable of change, is not only at the heart of Christianity and Quakerism but is the basis for Gandhian nonviolence.

Faith and reality

But is such belief fanciful or incapable of being put into action? I have long been convinced that if Jesus' teaching or Quaker beliefs were to be taken seriously, as a way to follow rather than a neverland to escape to, it was a philosophical necessity to understand that the world will actually work best for humanity according to the principles they embody. While I was writing my book I found good evidence from archaeological anthropology that war was not just a "fact" of human existence to which we were doomed by nature, and that co-operation and altruism were vital human capacities.*

Not only is altruism part of who we are: acting violently is a violation of our own deepest humanity. Can you imagine setting about the business of killing someone, or even training to do it? It is all too easy to feel uncertainty, in theory, about abolishing war, but how many of us would be able to participate? A former lieutenant in the US Army, S L A Marshall, after intensive research among fighting forces, wrote, "Fear of killing, rather than fear of being killed, was the most common cause of battle failure in the individual" (Dan Baum 2004). Killing is

---

* See, for example, Riane Eisler (1990) and Raymond Kelly (2000).

contrary to the norms we live by and, from our experience, to the spirit that is at the heart of our nature as human beings.

This evidence about human nature confirms my belief that when Jesus talked about turning the other cheek, going the extra mile and giving away your shirt as well as your coat he was talking not simply about what was right to do but what would work (Walter Wink 1987). It was based on the notion of human beings as essentially moral and morality as the basis for human society.

Then recently I read a most excellent Quaker pamphlet: George Ellis's *Science in Faith and Hope* (2004). George presents just such a point of view, describing it as "moral realism". From this perspective "deep ethics" is not invented but "discovered": a universal system "invariant across time and space". I believe that life is self-affirming and that this deep ethics is one aspect of the spirit that is present in all of us, which we experience in many ways, in different moments and contexts, and in whose presence we find ourselves in meeting for worship. It is one with the creative energy that brings growth and healing out of destruction and that can break the spiral of violence.

The function of faith is not to overcome reason but to take us into places where reason alone is not enough. I believe that reason should tell us that systematised killing and reliance on violence and the threat of violence can never be a satisfactory way of conducting human affairs or upholding human values. Reason can tell us that humanity is currently heading in a very dangerous direction and is in desperate need of spiritual grounding of a kind that upholds respect and tenderness and rejects violence. Faith can assure us that if we make the break with violence we will find that our capacity for ensuring each other's safety will be enhanced rather than diminished – and will also become less needed. Reason can tell us that resources not consumed by militarism can make possible the eradication of the poverty that destroys even more lives than war does. Faith can give us the sense of possibility that can generate the will for this to happen.

Where should we start?

In his opening chapter, Brian discussed what he saw as the distinctive qualities of contemporary global witness: identifying those who can make a change; a ministry of presence; continuity of commitment;

acts of faith; and a pragmatic approach (in the context of his chapter this was applied to reconciliation).

The first people we have to identify as able to make a change are ourselves, and the first place where we need to be present is in our own society and communities. We can also seek connections with others: both people we recognise as heading in the same direction as we are, with whom we can build alliances, and those whose perspective, position and sphere of influence is very different from our own but with whose human spirit we can find resonance. And we can work for global coalitions to address global problems. Taking a pragmatic approach and watching out for entry points and growth points will help us to use our energy strategically and so to be effective.

Continuity of commitment is essential. We have a historic testimony to peace, supported by other testimonies that give peace a profile. Can we maintain this undertaking, despite our differences and uncertainties; also despite discouragement and weariness? This is where faith comes in. Is our faith sufficient to sustain us?

This is a book about Quaker "witness" – not "work" or "action" – though we see that much work and action are involved. Witnessing, in this sense, means testifying to something within our experience. There is also an older meaning of "witness" as a noun, from which this verbal meaning came: "knowledge, understanding, wisdom". We witness to what we know. And this is the very heart of Quakerism: inner, "experimental" knowledge of the spirit.

I heartily agree with Charles Carter, as quoted by Diana and John Lampen, that there can be a dangerous illusion of Quaker uniqueness and that "it may be that Quakerism will not regain its effectiveness until we have learned to be ashamed of the proud myth of our uniqueness". When I encounter the commitment to peace and justice of many of my non-Quaker colleagues and fellow campaigners, I think that this is so. Our faith is perhaps the only special thing we can bring.

We live in a climate that is inimical to faith: one of great existential uncertainty, to which fanaticism and despair are all too often the alternatives. Do we expect our faith to make a difference? Is it the basis of our life and action or a comfort blanket in the chaos? Dare we find out? Are we willing to take the risk of talking to each other, openly and seriously, about our faith and lack of it? Do we dare to expose our differences in order to find our common ground? Do we have the commitment to act to the outer limits of our beliefs, whatever they are, rather than staying on safe ground? "More of the same" does not seem a sustainable option for human society or for our planet. Perhaps that commitment can help put risk in perspective and whatever can support risk-taking at a premium.

Do we trust the spirit to infuse us with a faith that is not self-indulgent or foolhardy but which will supply an ingredient that our world desperately needs? Do we dare to open ourselves to that spirit? Those Friends who have had the courage to translate their peacemaking beliefs into action have experienced their confirmation and felt the spirit at work – whether at a military base or in the mediation centre, working for change at home or supporting people in countries far away. Can we be open to learning from each other's experiences and let them nourish our faith?

An Ecumenical Accompanier helps a Palestinian woman with English

I am convinced that our belief in the human spirit is the most important thing we have to offer. I am also convinced that faithfulness will lead to a renewal of faith. I believe that if we open ourselves to our experience of the spirit in the silence of worship we shall recognise that spirit not only as peace but as power for growth in human kindness and as joy, hope and vision. Where there is no vision the people perish (Proverbs 29:18). With vision, pragmatism and commitment, we can play our part in the global movement for peace founded on justice and respect: for change that is indeed possible, if only we believe in it enough.

In the words of the 1987 Epistle of Friends in Aotearoa/New Zealand:

> Together, let us reject the clamour of fear and listen to the whisperings of hope. Stand up and be counted for what is no less than the affirmation of life and the destiny of humankind.

(Quaker Faith & Practice 24.10)

Five defining qualities of Quaker global witness in the Twenty-first century

- ■ Identifying those who can make a change
- ■ A ministry of presence
- ■ Continuity of commitment
- ■ Acts of faith
- ■ Pragmatic approaches to reconciliation

Be patterns, be examples, in all countries, places, islands, nations, wherever you come, that your carriage and life may preach among all sorts of people, and to them; then you will come to walk cheerfully over the world, answering that of God in every one.

George Fox in 1656 (*Quaker Faith & Practice* 19.32)

True godliness don't turn men out of the world but enables them to live better in it and excites their endeavours to mend it ... Christians should keep the helm and guide the vessel to its port; not meanly steal out at the stern of the world and leave those that are in it without a pilot to be driven by the fury of evil times upon the rock or sand of ruin.

William Penn in 1682 (*Quaker Faith & Practice* 23.02)

References and further reading

Works referred to in this book

Abbott, Margery Post & Parsons, Peggy Senger: *Walk Worthy of your Calling*, Richmond, Indiana: Friends United Press, 2004

Barclay, A R: *Letters &c of Early Friends*, London: Harvey & Darton, 1841

Baum, Dan: "The Price of Valor", *The New Yorker*, July 12 & 19, 2004

Bonhoeffer, Dietrich: *The Cost of Discipleship*, New York: Macmillan, 1963

Bonhoeffer, Dietrich: *Letters and Papers from Prison*, New York: Simon and Schuster, 1997

Braithwaite, William: *Spiritual Guidance in the experience of the Society of Friends*, London Yearly Meeting, 1909 (Swarthmore Lecture)

Brett, Rachel & McCallin, Margaret: *Children the Invisible Soldiers*, Stockholm: Rädda Barnen, 1996 (2nd edition 1998)

Brett, Rachel & Specht, Irma: *Young Soldiers: Why They Choose to Fight*, Geneva, ILO & Boulder, Colorado: Lynne Rienner, 2004

Cadbury, Henry: *John Woolman in England*, London: Friends Historical Society, 1971

Carter, Charles C: review of Roger C Wilson: *Quaker Relief 1940–1948*, London: *The Friend* 25.7.1952

Chechnya in my Heart, Karta journal, 1997. Some copies are available in English: contact cpcd-uk@supanet.com

Dandelion, Ben Pink, Gwyn, Douglas & Peat, Timothy: *Heaven on Earth: Quakers and the Second Coming*, Kelso and Birmingham: Curlew Productions and Woodbrooke College, 1998

Eisler, Riane: *The Chalice and the Blade: Our History, Our Future*, London: Unwin Paperbacks, 1990

Ellis, George: *Science in Faith and Hope: an interaction*, London: Quaker Books, 2004

European Centre for Conflict Prevention: *People Making Peace II*, Boulder, Colorado: Lynne Rienner, 2005

Fisher, Simon: *Spirited Living: Waging Conflict, Building Peace*, London: Quaker Books, 2004 (Swarthmore Lecture)

Fox, George: *Journal*, ed John Nickalls, London: Religious Society of Friends, 1975; reprinted Philadelphia Yearly Meeting and Quaker Home Service, 1997

Francis, Diana: *People, Peace and Power: Conflict Transformation in Action*, London: Pluto Press, 2002

Francis, Diana: *Rethinking War and Peace*, London: Pluto Press, 2004

Greenwood, J Ormerod: *Vines on the Mountains*, York: Sessions, 1977

Hulot, Nicholas & Sipa-Press: *Ces Enfants qui souffrent*, Paris: PAC, 1978

Katana, Gordana: "Republika Srpska Sanctions Threat" in *Balkan Crisis Reports*, Issue 245, 10 May 2001, London: Institute for War and Peace Reporting, available at www.iwpr.net

Keairns, Yvonne E: *The Voices of Girl Child Soldiers*: Summary, October 2002; *The Voices of Girl Child Soldiers*: Colombia, January 2003; *The Voices of Girl Child Soldiers*: Philippines, January 2003; and *The Voices of Girl Child Soldiers*: Sri Lanka, January 2003, QUNO Geneva jointly with QUNO New York

Kelly, Raymond: *Warless Societies and the Origin of War*, Ann Arbor, Michigan: University of Michigan Press, 2000

Lampen, John: *Will Warren – a scrapbook*, London: Quaker Home Service, 1983

Liveoak, Val: "Quaker Practices and Processes for Peacemaking" in *Peace Teams News*, Hyattsville, Maryland: Friends Peace Teams, Spring 2003

Nayler, James: *Works*, London, 1716

Prys-Williams, Barbara: "Handing on Madagascar", London: *The Friend*, 14.6.1996

Quaker Faith & Practice: the book of Christian discipline of the Yearly Meeting of the Religious Society of Friends (Quakers) in Britain (QFP), London: Britain Yearly Meeting, 1994; 3rd edition 2005

Quaker Peace & Service: "Guidelines for Interest Groups of the World Regional Programme Committee", London: Britain Yearly Meeting, 10.8.1999

Quaker Peace & Social Witness: "Review and Evaluation of QPSW Northern Uganda Project", London: Britain Yearly Meeting, December 2002

Raistrick, Arthur: *Quakers in Science and Industry*, Newton Abbot: David & Charles, 1968

Rose, June: *Elizabeth Fry*, London: Quaker Home Service, 1994

Sewel, William: *History of the Rise, Increase, and Progress of the . . . Quakers*, London, 1722, vol. I

Solerland, Jean: "African Americans and Native Americans in John Woolman's World" in Mike Heller (ed): *Tendering Presence:*

Essays on John Woolman, Wallingford, Pennsylvania: Pendle Hill, 2003

Townsend, Peter: *The Smallest Pawns in the Game*, London: Granada, 1980

Williams, Rowan: *Christ on Trial: How the Gospel Unsettles our Judgment*, London: HarperCollins, 2000

Wilson, Roger C: *Authority, Leadership and Concern*, London: George Allen & Unwin, 1949; repr. Friends Home Service Committee, 1970 (Swarthmore Lecture)

Wilson, Roger C: "Relief and Reconstruction" in John Kavanaugh (ed), *The Quaker Approach to Contemporary Problems*, London: George Allen and Unwin, 1953

Wink, Walter: *Jesus' Third Way: Violence and Nonviolence in South Africa*, Philadelphia: New Society Publishers, 1987

Woolman, John: *Works*, Philadelphia, 1774

Woolman, John: *The Journal and Major Essays*, ed Phillips Moulton, Richmond, Indiana: Friends United Press, 1989

Further reading

Action for Conflict Transformation (eds.). *Transforming Conflict: reflections of practitioners worldwide*. Action for Conflict Transformation, 2003

Bailey, Sydney. *Peace Is a Process*. Quaker Books, 1993, ISBN 0852452497

Curle, Adam. *True Justice: Quaker Peacemakers and Peace Making*. Quaker Books, 1981, ISBN 0852451563

Fisher, Simon, et al. *Working with Conflict: skills and strategies for action*. Zed Books, 2000, ISBN 1 856 49837 9

Fisher, Simon. *Spirited Living: Waging Conflict, Building Peace*. Quaker Books, 2004, ISBN 0852453574

Francis, Diana. *People, Peace and Power: Conflict Transformation in Action*. Pluto Press, 2002, ISBN 0745318355

Francis, Diana. *Rethinking War and Peace*. Pluto Press, 2004, ISBN 0745321879

Lampen, John (ed.). *No Alternative: Nonviolent Responses to Repressive Regimes*. York: Sessions Book Trust, 2000, ISBN 1850722439

Large, Judith. *The War Next Door: Study of Second Track Interventions During the War in Ex-Yugoslavia*. Stroud: Hawthorn Press, 1997, ISBN 1869890973

Lederach, John Paul. *Building Peace: sustainable reconciliation in divided societies.* Washington, DC: United States Institute of Peace Press, 1997, ISBN 1878379739

Lederach, John Paul. *The Moral Imagination: The Art and Soul of Building Peace.* New York: Oxford University Press, 2004, ISBN 0195174542

Mendl, Wolf. *Prophets and Reconcilers: Reflections on the Quaker Peace Testimony.* Friends Home Service, 1974, ISBN 0852451156

Schell, Jonathan. *The Unconquerable World: Power, Nonviolence and the Will of the People.* Allen Lane, 2004, ISBN 0713997664

Steven, Helen. *No Extraordinary Power: Prayer, Stillness and Activism.* Quaker Books, 2005, ISBN 0852453795

Van Tongeren, Paul, et al (eds.). *People Building Peace IT successful stories of civil society.* Boulder, CO: Lynne Rienner, 2005, ISBN 1588263835

Websites

The Hope Project: www.hopeproject.co.uk
The European Peacebuilding Liaison Office: www.eplo.org

Index

Index

Index